"Wisdom That Transforms. Action That Lasts."

The Get Wisdom Commitment

At Get Wisdom Publishing we believe that true wisdom has the power to transform lives. Our mission is to equip readers with timeless insights and practical tools that inspire growth, guide decisions, and empower purposeful living. We don't just inform—we empower.

Our books combine profound understanding with real-life application, enabling readers to unlock their potential and navigate life's challenges with clarity and confidence. With each step guided by wisdom, we help you create lasting change and live the life you deserve.

When wisdom meets purpose, transformation follows.

Walk in all the ways the Lord has commanded!

Copyright

ISBN   978-1-952359-64-4   (paperback)
ISBN   978-1-952359-65-1   (ebook)

This book is available as an audiobook on our Amazon Jesus Follower Series page:	

Unlock Biblical Wisdom and Transform Your Faith

**For more information
about the Jesus Follower Bible Study Series:**
https://getwisdompublishing.com/jesus-follower-series/

Walk in all the ways the Lord has commanded!

Jesus Follower Bible Study Series

The OBEDIENCE Requirements For a Jesus Follower

Ignore At Your Own Risk!

Stephen H Berkey

GETWISDOM PUBLISHING

This book is available as an audiobook on our Amazon Jesus Follower Series page:

Free PDF
Living Wisely

The Life Planning Guide

A Quick-Start Guide to Purposeful Living and Wise Decisions!

Discover the five life domains: purpose, people, principles, productivity, and perspective. Wisdom is the ability to apply truth and logic to real-life decisions and produce good outcomes. It influences your choices and will produce action that lasts. Consider and apply the five practical wisdom principles for daily living. (6 pages)

Free PDF: https://getwisdompublishing.com/resource-registration/

Living Wisely
The Life Planning Guide

Wisdom That Transforms.
Action That Lasts.

Stephen H Berkey
J.S. Wellman

Free PDF

Five Practical Principles For Life

When wisdom meets purpose, transformation follows.

Free PDF
Wise Decision-Making

[Get the ebook version for 99 cents]

You can make good choices.

This free resource provides a project-oriented perspective and gives ten detailed steps to analyze issues/problems to determine a solution. (26 pages)

Good decisions expand your horizons. Don't allow the fear of decision-making paralyze your ability to make good choices. Think through the reasonable alternatives and move forward. When your eyes are on the goal, making good decisions is easier.

Free PDF: https://getwisdompublishing.com/resource-registration/

Kindle ebook for 99 cents: https://www.amazon.com/dp/B09SYGWRVL/

Ebook

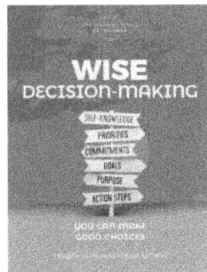

Free PDF

Make Thoughtful Decisions!

Good decisions expand your horizons.

The Jesus Follower Journey
Jesus Follower Bible Study Series

The Jesus Follower Bible Study Series will provide you with a complete description of the nature, characteristics, obligations, commitments, and responsibilities of a true Jesus follower.

Go to our Amazon Book Series page for your copy:
https://www.amazon.com/dp/B0DHP39P5J

The RELATIONSHIP CHARACTERISTICS of a Jesus Follower:
    Are you right with God?
The ONE ANOTHER INSTRUCTIONS to a Jesus Follower:
    Are you right with one another?
The WORSHIP of a Jesus Follower:
    Is your worship acceptable or in vain?
The PRAYER of a Jesus Follower:
    What Scripture says about unleashing the power of God.
The DANGERS of SIN for a Jesus Follower:
    God HATES sin! He abhors sin!
The FOCUS for a Jesus Follower:
    Keep your eyes fixed on Jesus!
The HEART Requirements of a Jesus Follower:
    Follow with all your heart, mind, body, and soul!
The COMMITMENTS of a Jesus Follower:
    Practical Christian living and discipleship.
The OBEDIENCE Requirements for a Jesus Follower:
    Ignore at your own risk!

A related book to this series is, *Effective Life Change: Applying Biblical Wisdom to Live Your Best Life!* This book offers a practical and powerful guide to help navigate life's challenges based on the proverbial wisdom of the Bible. It offers ten commitments hat will profoundly change your life.

Effective Life Change
Applying Biblical Wisdom to Live Your Best Life!

Why Read This Book?

- Transform Your life with Biblical Wisdom.
- Cultivate Practical Wisdom in Your life.
- Navigate Life with a Perspective on Biblical Truth.
- Unlock the Proverbs of the Bible to Live Your Best Life.
- Change and Transform Your life.

   Practical Application: These aren't theology or religious discussions, they're practical tools for everyday living.

Get Your Copy Today!

https://www.amazon.com/dp/1952359732
Available in Hardcover, Paperback, Kindle, and Audiobook.

Table of Contents

For the Lord gives wisdom;
from his mouth come knowledge
and understanding; he stores up
sound wisdom for the upright;
he is a shield to those
who walk in integrity,

Proverbs 2:6-7 ESV

"Get Wisdom Publishing creates wisdom-driven
products that equip readers with timeless
insights, understanding, and actionable
tools to transform their lives."

Message From the Author

Dear Fellow Christ follower,

Welcome to a journey of faith and discovery.

As the author of this Bible study series, I am excited about the future because I believe this book provides the potential to transform lives, deepen our understanding of God's Word, and ignite a desire within us—a fire that draws us into the presence of our God.

Why read the Jesus Follower Series?

Deeper Roots: We all long for roots that run deep—roots anchored in truth, love, and purpose. In this series, we'll dig into the bedrock of Scripture, unearthing spiritual principles that will guide us in our faith journey.

Authentic Discipleship: Being a Jesus follower isn't about rituals or a superficial commitment. It's about walking the narrow path, picking up your cross, and living a life that loves God, follows Jesus, and loves one another. We will explore what it means to be authentic disciples.

Unveiling Mysteries: God is a source of mysteries and His Word is waiting to be discovered. Together we will examine and encounter the living Word—the One who breathes life into every syllable.

Community and Connection: We are not meant to walk this path alone. As you read, imagine joining a global community of fellow seekers. We will discuss, question, and grow together. Our shared journey will enrich us all. I encourage you to gather friends to join you in this journey.

Expected Benefits:

Renewed Passion: Prepare yourself to wake up each morning with a renewed passion for God's Word. These studies will ignite your hunger for truth and draw you into deeper relationship with the Author of Life.

Practical Application: These aren't theoretical discussions; they're practical tools for everyday living. Expect to see real-life changes—whether it's in your relationships, commitment, or prayer life.

Spiritual Resilience: Life's storms will come, but armed with the insights from God's Word, you can stand firm. Your faith will weather trials, doubts, and uncertainties. You will emerge stronger and more resilient.

Joyful Obedience: As we explore the nature of discipleship, you'll discover that obedience isn't a burden—it's a joy. The path of obedience leads to peace, and you'll find yourself saying, "Yes, Lord!" with newfound delight.

Let's Begin!

So, turn the page. Dive into the first chapter. Let the words seep into your soul. And remember, you're not alone—we're on this pilgrimage together. May these books be more than ink on paper; may they be stepping stones toward a life that leads to eternity. Amen!

"We believe applied wisdom empowers life change. Our books provide clarity, inspiration, and tools to equip readers to live their best life."

My prayer is that you will

Be tenacious like Job
Walk like Enoch
Believe like Abraham
Wrestle like Jacob
Dress like Joseph
Lead like Moses
Conquer like Deborah
Be fearless like Shamgar
Inspire like Josuha
Influence like Esther
Dance like David
Ask like Jabez
Have the faith of Daniel
Pray like Elijah
Trust like Elisha
Commit like Isaiah
Be courageous like Benaiah
Rebuild like Nehemiah
Be obedient like Hosea
Be zealous like Zacchaeus
Surrender like Mary
Stand firm like Stephen
Speak like Peter
Seize opportunities like Philip
Submit like Paul
Overcome like the Elect (Saints)
Worship like the 24 Elders
and
Love like Jesus

Steve

Introduction

Book Description

Are you ready to take your faith to the next level? This book is a compelling, eye-opening study that challenges you to examine the true meaning of obedience in your walk with Christ. This book is not just a theoretical discussion. It's a call to action.

In a world where compromise is common, we dare to ask the tough questions: How serious is God about obeying His commands? What are the consequences of disobedience in our lives? Can we truly overcome temptation and sin? Can our disobedience impact our salvation?

The focus will be on the Scriptures as we explore:

The Fundamentals of Obedience: Uncover what it really means to live in alignment with God's will.
Obedience and Salvation: Examine the critical link between following God's commands and eternal life.
Punishment for Disobedience: What does it mean when you rebel against God's laws?
The Fear of the Lord: Discover how this often-misunderstood concept transforms your relationship with God.
Standing Firm: Learn practical strategies to resist the enemy and persevere in faith.

Through engaging lessons and biblical examples, you'll gain a new appreciation for the power of obedience and its impact on your spiritual growth. This study doesn't just present theory—it equips you with the tools to boldly live out your faith with confidence. Each lesson is designed to challenge your understanding and inspire you to embrace a life of faithful obedience.

The most profound truth you'll discover is that obedience is not just a duty but a gateway to a deeper, more intimate relationship with God through Christ. If you're serious about following Jesus, this study will equip you with the knowledge, understanding, and spiritual resilience to walk in obedience—no matter the cost.

Are you tired of lukewarm faith? Do you long for a deeper, more authentic relationship with God? This is your roadmap to a life of purpose, power, and unwavering faith. Through compelling biblical examples and practical applications, you will see how people like Moses and Paul exemplified obedience in their lives. You can do the same.

This study will empower you to confront the challenges of disobedience and encourage you to cultivate a deeper relationship with God through Christ.

Don't settle for less than God's best for your life. Embrace the challenge of obedience and watch as your faith comes alive like never before.

Group Discussion or Individual Study

These studies can be done individually or in a small discussion group. An important value of the study is in the discussion questions. We all see life differently and the thoughts and ideas shared in a group will often lead to a richer understanding of the Scripture. We recommend doing these studies in a group, if possible.

Format of Lessons

The format of the lessons is not the same in each book. We chose a format that best fit the material.

We Reap What We Sow!

In a number of his proverbs, King Solomon suggests that doing what is right is to be preferred over evil. King Solomon was known world-wide for his great wisdom. He wrote and recorded many proverbs recognized for their practical insight and wisdom. He describes the nature of righteousness as being immovable and that it will stand above evil.

Is your desire for doing what is "right" rooted deeply or is it planted in shallow soil that can easily be washed away? Solomon indicated that the wicked would ultimately be overthrown and that the righteous would survive because their character had roots that were deep and impossible to dislodge.

Solomon argued that it was better to be on the side of the righteous. The reasoning is the same as the man who builds his house, business, or life on rock versus sand. If we build on sand (questionable ways) then our hopes and plans will never stand up against the storms of life. If we build on rock (character, commitment, and obedience) our plans will hold firm.

We do reap what we sow and if we sow badly because we have rejected what is right, the wise counsel of friends, or our core values, we will reap the negative consequences. Those who think they know everything frequently reject wisdom and follow their own plans and schemes. It has been said that those who insist on following their own foolish ways will often end up choking on them.

Lesson 1
The Fundamentals of Obedience

OBEDIENCE

Obedience is not a very popular word in our society today! In today's culture we will be more readily accepted if we are tolerant, compromising, lenient, and relational. Society wants us to see everything as relative. In other words, keep everybody happy and satisfied, there is no absolute truth, and if I am not directly bothering you, then I can do anything I please. But that approach to life is not consistent with the Christian faith.

God clearly calls us to be obedient to His Word. Generally there can be no spiritual growth, no godly empowering, and no effective ministry without obedience. Rebellion (*sin*) is surely the primary reason for the lack of spiritual authority and intimacy with God in many homes and churches today.

Rebellion in the Biblical context occurs when we choose to do our own thing or create our own personal or corporate standards and values, contrary to the commands of God.

> **Isaiah 30:1** *"Ah, stubborn children," declares the Lord, "who carry out a plan, but not mine, and who make an alliance, but not of my Spirit, that they may add sin to sin."* ESV
> [This is one of the six "woes" Isaiah delivered to the nation of Israel, ending with judgment in Isaiah 34.]

But as much as the Lord hates rebellion, He stands up for obedience:

> **Isaiah 1:19-20** *If you are willing and obedient, you shall eat the good of the land; 20 but if you refuse and rebel, you shall be eaten by the sword; for the mouth of the Lord has spoken.* ESV

At the very heart of our relationship with God lies obedience to His commandments. Obedience must be a fundamental foundation of our walk with God, even our very existence. We must do things His way, trusting in His plan for our lives. Obedience must be a constant and continual desire of our heart. The imperfect results of even our most strenuous efforts reveals the necessity of God's grace provided at the Cross.[1]
(see 1 John 1:6-10; 2:1-6; Romans 3:20; 5:1; 6:1-2.)

In both the Old and New Testaments the word "obey" is frequently related to the idea of hearing. Obedience, then, should be an active response to what a person hears. God summons people to active obedience in His revelations and man's failure to obey is *sin* which results in God's judgment.

In the Old Testament covenant between God and man, obedience was the basis for knowing God's blessing and favor (Exodus 19:5; 24:1-8). Samuel emphasized that God's pleasure was not in sacrifice but in obedience (1 Samuel 15:22). Even the promise of a new covenant emphasized that the people broke the covenant. (Jeremiah 31:31ff).[2]

TRUST and OBEY

Does this heading remind you of a song title? It should. "Trust and Obey" was written by John Henry Sammis in

1887, with music composed by Daniel Brink Towner. Examining the lyrics should be helpful as we begin this journey to understand the meaning and nature of living in obedience to God's teaching.

Verse 1: When we walk with the Lord In the light of His Word, What a glory He sheds on our way; While we do His good will, He abides with us still, And with all who will trust and obey.

> Refrain: Trust and obey,
> For there's no other way
> To be happy in Jesus,
> But to trust and obey.

Verse 2: Not a shadow can rise, Not a cloud in the skies, But His smile quickly drives it away; Not a doubt or a fear, Not a sigh or a tear, Can abide while we trust and obey. [Refrain]

Verse 3: Not a burden we bear, Not a sorrow we share, But our toil He doth richly repay; Not a grief or a loss, Not a frown or a cross, But is blest if we trust and obey. [Refrain]

Verse 4: But we never can prove The delights of His love Until all on the altar we lay; For the favor He shows, And the joy He bestows, Are for them who will trust and obey. [Refrain]

Verse 5: Then in fellowship sweet We will sit at His feet, Or we'll walk by His side in the way; What He says we will do, Where He sends we will go; Never fear, only trust and obey. [Refrain]

Q1. In verse 1 what are we to do?

(a)

(b)

(c)

Q2. What does God do in verse 1?

(a)

(b)

Q3. What assurance is provided in verse 2?

(a)

(b)

Q4. What does God do when we trust and obey in verse 3?

(a)

(b)

Q5. If we trust and obey in verse 4, what do we do?

(a)

(b)

(c)

Q6. What are we to do other than trust and obey in verse 4?

Q7. Based on the Refrain, what is it we get if we trust and obey?

Q8. Consider the words of this song. What strikes you about the lyrics?

A SUPREME TEST OF FAITH

Obedience may be the supreme test of faith. In the Old Testament it was the required condition for maintaining a right relationship with God. This is most clearly stated in the relationship between Abraham and Yahweh when Abraham is assured by God: "*and in your offspring shall all the nations of the earth be blessed, because you have obeyed my voice.*" (Genesis 22:18 ESV)

In most prophecy or commandments, blessings and judgment are conditioned upon obedience: "*If you are willing and obedient, you shall eat the good of the land*" (Isaiah 1:19 ESV). After describing the glories of the coming Messianic kingdom, the prophets would assure the people that such blessings would only occur if the people would diligently obey their God (Zechariah 6:15). On the other hand misfortune, calamity, distress, or famine might come because of disobedience.

In the New Testament a higher spiritual and moral relationship is suggested as compared to the Old Testament, but the importance of obedience was still greatly emphasized. Christ Himself demonstrated His obedience by going to the Cross. He humbled himself, being obedient to the Father, even unto death (Philippians 2:8). By obedience to His teaching we receive the salvation provided by His sacrifice (Hebrews 5:9).

"Obedience of faith" is a term used by Paul to express this idea (Romans 1:5). Peter describes believers in Christ as "children of obedience" (1 Peter 1:14). The test of a relationship with Yahweh in the Old Testament is performance obedience. The relationship with Christ in the New Testament is obedience through faith and God's gift of grace.[3]

Thus a right relationship with God requires obedience, by which we become identified as a disciple of Christ. The Gospel of John indicates that Jesus also considers *love* a requirement because that defines a disciple: *"A new commandment I give to you, that you love one another: just as I have loved you, you also are to love one another. 35 By this all people will know that you are my disciples, if you have love for one another."* (John 13:34-35 ESV)

Q9. What does John say about obedience in the following verses:

John 14:15

John 14:23

1 John 5:3

HOW TO DO IT?

What, if anything, can produce obedience in our lives? At first glance obedience to a holy and righteous God seems a bit daunting! But Peter says that we were chosen for obedience:

> *. . . who* [God's people] *have been <u>chosen</u> according to the foreknowledge of God the Father, through the sanctifying work of the Spirit, <u>for obedience to Jesus Christ</u> and sprinkling by his blood* . . .(1 Peter 1:2 NIV)

If it is true that I was chosen for obedience and am one of the Elect (chosen by God), then He knows I am capable of the obedience He desires. Therefore, I must believe that He has told us in His Word how to achieve such obedience. Let's look at what the following passages say about how to demonstrate that obedience.

Q10. What do we learn about <u>how</u> to obey in the following:

Hebrews 5:8 _____

Although he was a son, he learned obedience through what he suffered. ESV

Philippians 2:8_____

And being found in human form, he humbled himself by becoming obedient to the point of death, even death on a cross. ESV

John 15:10 _____

If you keep my commandments, you will abide in my love, just as I have kept my Father's commandments and abide in his love. ESV

Romans 1:5 _____

through whom we have received grace and apostleship to bring about the obedience of faith for the sake of his name among all the nations. ESV

Ephesians 5:6 _____

Let no one deceive you with empty words, for because of these things the wrath of God comes upon the sons of disobedience. ESV [also see 1 Peter 4:17 and 2 Thessalonians 1:8]

John 14:15 _____

If you love me, you will keep my commandments. ESV

Q11. How would you summarize what these revelations about learning to be obedient mean to you personally?

WISDOM OF THE PROVERBS

Remember that the proverbs in the Bible are not absolute truth but rather practical wisdom for daily living that are true in general. They are produced from observing how life really works and drawing astute conclusions. They offer practical advice that can be relied on as general truth. As indicated in Proverbs 15:24 they can even be used to discern the path of life in order to avoid hell.

The following verses from Proverbs emphasize the value of obedience for living according to wisdom and instruction, highlighting the blessings and benefits that come from making good life choices.

Q12. What do we learn about obedience in the following proverbs?

Proverbs 3:5-6 *Trust in the Lord with all your heart, and do not lean on your own understanding. 6 In all your ways acknowledge him, and he will make straight your paths.* ESV

Proverbs 28:9 *If one turns away his ear from hearing the law, even his prayer is an abomination.* ESV

Proverbs 19:20 *Listen to advice and accept instruction, that you may gain wisdom in the future.* ESV

Proverbs 1:7 *The fear of the Lord is the beginning of knowledge; fools despise wisdom and instruction.* ESV

Proverbs 15:32 *Whoever ignores instruction despises himself, but he who listens to reproof gains intelligence.* ESV

Proverbs 10:8 *The wise of heart will receive commandments, but a babbling fool will come to ruin.* ESV

Proverbs 16:20 *Whoever gives thought to the word will discover good, and blessed is he who trusts in the Lord.* ESV

Proverbs 4:13 *Keep hold of instruction; do not let go; guard her, for she is your life.* ESV

In the Proverbs that instruct people to obey God or His instructions, several major themes or categories of commands can be identified. These themes reflect foundational principles of righteous living and gaining wisdom, even from correction and reproof. These principles are consistently emphasized throughout the book of Proverbs. They provide practical guidance for living a life that is pleasing to God and bring blessings to the one who conforms to the advice.

Here are the major categories:

Fear of the Lord
Several proverbs emphasize the fear of the Lord as the beginning of wisdom, understanding, and knowledge (Proverbs 1:7, 9:10). This theme underscores the fundamental importance of God as the source of knowledge and wisdom.

Seeking Wisdom
The Proverbs frequently encourage individuals to seek wisdom and understanding (Proverbs 2:1-6). This inherently requires pursuing knowledge and understanding of God's ways. Romans 12:2 instructs us to renew our minds so we can discern His will. Knowing His will leads to making wise choices and living righteously.

Living Righteously
The Proverbs provide numerous instructions on how to live a righteous and upright life. This means we should avoid evil (Proverbs 3:7), be honest and truthful (Proverbs 12:22), and practice justice and kindness (Proverbs 21:3).

Receiving Instruction
The importance of receiving and accepting instruction or correction is a major recurring theme. This means we listen to wise counsel (Proverbs 19:20), accept discipline (Proverbs 3:11-12), and are open to correction (Proverbs 15:31-32).

Guarding the Heart
Proverbs emphasizes the need to guard one's heart and mind against sinful influences and temptations. This means we should avoid sinful companions (Proverbs 13:20). We must also control our speech (Proverbs 21:23) and cultivate a wise and discerning heart (Proverbs 4:23).

Honoring God with Wealth

Proverbs provides practical advice about the proper use of wealth. We should be generous to the poor (Proverbs 19:17) and trust in God's provision (Proverbs 3:9-10).

Maintaining Humility

Being humble and avoiding arrogance is repeated as a virtue throughout Proverbs. This means acknowledging one's dependence on God (Proverbs 3:5-6) and being open to wisdom (Proverbs 15:33).

Seeking Peace and Harmony

The final category is to encourage people to pursue peace and harmony in their relationships. This means we should avoid strife (Proverbs 17:14) and speak words of kindness and reconciliation (Proverbs 15:1).

CONCLUSION

God desires that we live our lives well and with honor. Scripture strongly encourages us to live righteously in many ways. The advice of Proverbs is particularly helpful in living life wisely.

If you struggle with making the right decisions about life and relationships, start reading one chapter of Proverbs each day. There are 31 chapters, thus you can read through the book each month until the advice becomes second nature in your thinking.

The book of Proverbs serves as an invaluable resource for gaining wisdom, living a life of integrity, and honoring God in all our endeavors. Its practical advice will benefit you regardless of your age and circumstances. Its wisdom is timeless and it transcends cultural and historical bias. Thus, it is applicable to individuals in different stages of life and diverse cultural settings.

Here are five reasons to read and study Proverbs:

1. **Wisdom for Daily Life:** The Proverbs provides practical advice for overcoming many of the challenges of life, including relationships, work, finances, speech, etc.

2. **Foundation for Values:** Proverbs emphasize the importance of living with integrity, righteousness, and in fear of the Lord. It lays a strong foundation for moral values which align with God's standards.

3. **Understanding the Consequences of Actions:** The advice portrays the consequences of both wise and foolish behavior. Proverbs highlights the outcomes of different choices, allowing the reader to consider the consequences of their actions.

4. **Character Development:** Proverbs emphasizes the development of virtues such as humility, diligence, honesty, and self-control. By adopting these qualities, individuals grow in character and wisdom.

5. **Discernment and Disciplined Living:** Proverbs teaches the importance of discernment and disciplined living. It encourages readers to seek wisdom, and exercise sound judgment in all areas of life.

WHAT I WANT TO REMEMBER

Enter some notes and information that you want to remember about this lesson. It might be a Scripture verse or two, something new you learned, something you want to do, something you want to change, or just something you want to be sure to remember.

Wisdom to Action
Challenge

In what specific area of your life do you need to prioritize obedience to God's Word this week? How can you actively respond to His revelations in this area?

Lesson 2

Is Obedience *REALLY* Required by God?

INTRODUCTION

Does God really require absolute obedience? For many of us this may be the question we want to ask but are afraid to discuss. Maybe we don't want to know the answer! Or we are afraid to discuss it openly because it may imply we don't want to obey God's commands. We know we have ignored some of God's teaching and we don't want to talk about it – out of sight, out of mind. Or we would rather not begin a conversation about sin of any kind – past, present, or future. If we discuss it or share openly, others will think we are bigger sinners than they already assume. Or it's just a touchy subject that could lead to exposing our vulnerability and sinful nature.

Most people understand that partial obedience is not real obedience. For example, if we are told to cross the street and we only go 75% of the way, we have clearly not crossed the street. All you can claim is that you are in the street. James 2:10 says, *"For whoever keeps the whole law and yet stumbles at just one point is guilty of breaking all of it."*(NIV)

What is the nature of the obedience requirements, and what is the result of disobedience? Paul admitted to the world that his flesh did what his spirit did not want him to do, and he failed to do things he should have done. We see many other major characters in the Bible who failed to obey the laws of God.

There are large passages in Scripture, like Colossians 3, that tell us how to "walk" or "live" our lives. There are at least twenty categories of verses throughout the Bible that reveal to us the rules for holy living. These include instructions to live our lives: a) blameless, b) humble, c) in the light, d) in faith, e) in wisdom, f) in peace, g) in the Spirit, h) upright, and i) holy.

Each of these categories has multiple verses describing how we are to live this particular aspect in our Christian life. Thus, it would be hard to convince anyone knowledgeable about these verses that God does not expect obedience.

WHAT DOES SCRIPTURE SAY?

The basic question of this lesson is, "Does God really require absolute obedience?" Let's begin by answering the following questions about what Scripture says about obedience.

Q1. Does God accept partial obedience, given James 2:10?
James 2:10 *For whoever keeps the whole law but fails in one point has become accountable for all of it.* ESV

Q2. Does God expect us to obey based on the following?
1 Peter 1:2, 14 *God the Father knew you and chose you long ago, and his Spirit has made you holy. As a result, you have obeyed him and have been cleansed by the blood of Jesus Christ. . .14 So you must live as God's obedient*

children. Don't slip back into your old ways of living to satisfy your own desires. You didn't know any better then. NLT

Romans 1:5 *. . . through whom we have received grace and apostleship to bring about the obedience of faith for the sake of his name among all the nations.* ESV

Q3. Has obedience always been required?

Deuteronomy 10:12-13 Circumcise Your Heart

And now, Israel, what does the Lord your God require of you, but to fear the Lord your God, to walk in all his ways, to love him, to serve the Lord your God with all your heart and with all your soul, 13 and to keep the commandments and statutes of the Lord, which I am commanding you today for your good? ESV

Q4. What can we learn from looking at Jesus' life?

Philippians 2:8 *And being found in human form, he humbled himself by becoming obedient to the point of death, even death on a cross.* ESV

John 15:10 *If you keep my commandments, you will abide in my love, just as I have kept my Father's commandments and abide in his love.* ESV

Q5. Is obedience the common expectation in Bible teaching based on the following?

Our Parents:

Ephesians 6:1-2 *Children, obey your parents . . .*

Civil Authorities:

Romans 13:1, 7 Submission to the Authorities
Let every person be subject to the governing authorities. For there is no authority except from God, and those that exist have been instituted by God. . . . 7 Pay to all what is owed to them: taxes to whom taxes are owed, revenue to whom revenue is owed, respect to whom respect is owed, honor to whom honor is owed. ESV

Church:

Matthew 18:17 *If he refuses to listen to them, tell it to the church. And if he refuses to listen even to the church, let him be to you as a Gentile and a tax collector.* ESV

THE GREAT COMMANDMENT

The Great Commandment occurs in Matthew 22:36-40 and it is interesting to observe why Jesus responds in this manner. One of the disciples asked, "Teacher, which is the greatest commandment in the Law?" And Jesus gave the following answer:

Matthew 22:36-40 *"Teacher, which is the great commandment in the Law?" 37 And he said to him, "You shall love the Lord your God with all your heart and with all your soul and with all your mind. 38 This is the great and first commandment. 39 And a second is like it: You shall love your neighbor as yourself. 40 On these two commandments depend all the Law and the Prophets."* ESV

This command basically describes the foundational principle of Christian ethics and theology. Let's look closer at the meaning and implications of the two parts of this command.

First, we are to love God with all our heart, soul, and mind. This portion of the Great Commandment focuses on the importance of a deep and sincere love relationship with God.

Secondly, and probably as important as the first requirement, we are to love our neighbors as we love ourselves. This commandment highlights the importance of loving and caring for one another. It even sets the love bar equal to the way we love ourselves.

Q6. What does loving God with all your heart, soul, and mind mean to you?

Q7. How would you describe or explain the concept of loving others as yourself?

Overall, the Great Commandment captures the essence of the Christian faith. It serves as a guiding principle for how followers are called to live out their lives in relationship with God and with one another. There are some very important implications that we will highlight in the following questions.

Q8. What is the significance that love for God and one another are <u>both</u> part of the Great Commandment?

Q9. What does this Commandment say or imply about ethical living?

Q10. What does this Commandment say about the importance of the heart?

Q11. What does the Commandment imply about the mission of a Jesus follower?

Q12. What is the significance of Matthew 22:40 regarding the involvement of the "Law and the Prophets?"

WISDOM LITERATURE – Proverbs

In the Bible there are important commands that prescribe how followers are to act toward God and toward one another. Some of the most important ones include:

1. Divine Commands Toward God

Trust in the Lord
Proverbs 3:5-6 encourages believers to trust in the Lord with all their hearts. We are not to depend on our own understanding, but acknowledge God's sovereignty and wisdom in all aspects of life.

Fear of the Lord
The fear of the Lord is a recurring theme, emphasizing reverence, awe, and obedience to God. Proverbs 9:10 states, *"The fear of the Lord is the beginning of wisdom, and the knowledge of the Holy One is insight."* (ESV) In addition, there are similar proverbs describing the fear of the Lord and life:

> **Proverbs 10:27** *The fear of the Lord prolongs life, but the years of the wicked will be short.* ESV
> **Proverbs 14:27** *The fear of the Lord is a fountain of life, that one may turn away from the snares of death.* ESV
> **Proverbs 19:23** *The fear of the Lord leads to life, and whoever has it rests satisfied; he will not be visited by harm.* ESV

Q13. What is the message of Proverbs 3:6?

Proverbs 3:6 *"In all your ways acknowledge him, and he will make straight your paths."* ESV

2. Divine Commands Toward One Another

Practice Justice and Mercy:
Throughout the wisdom literature, there is an emphasis on acting justly and showing mercy toward one another:

> **Proverbs 21:3** *To do righteousness and justice is more acceptable to the Lord than sacrifice.* ESV
> **Proverbs 28:13** *Whoever conceals his transgressions will not prosper, but he who confesses and forsakes them will obtain mercy.* ESV

Be Humble
Humility is described as a desired virtue:

> **Proverbs 3:34** *Toward the scorners he is scornful, but to the humble he gives favor.* ESV
> **Proverbs 11:2** *When pride comes, then comes disgrace, but with the humble is wisdom.* ESV
> **Proverbs 22:4** *The reward for humility and fear of the Lord is riches and honor and life.* ESV

Q14. What does Proverbs 12:22 say about our speech?

Proverbs 12:22 *"Lying lips are an abomination to the Lord, but those who act faithfully are his delight."* ESV

These proverbial commands provide a framework for Christian living and discipleship, guiding believers in their relationship with God and their interactions with one another. They emphasize the importance of love, trust, obedience, honesty, justice, mercy, and humility in living out the principles of the Christian faith.

WISDOM LITERATURE – Psalms

The Psalms also provide important commands that outline how followers are to act toward God and toward one another:

1. Divine Commands Toward God

Praise and Worship
The Psalms contain many specific exhortations to praise and worship God. For example, Psalm 150:6 says, "*Let everything that has breath praise the Lord. Praise the Lord.*" ESV

Trust in God's Protection
Many Psalms express trust in God's protection and deliverance in times of trouble. For example, Psalm 91:2-4 says, "*I will say to the Lord, "My refuge and my fortress, my God, in whom I trust. 3 For he will deliver you from the snare of the fowler and from the deadly pestilence. 4 He will cover you with his pinions, and under his wings you will find refuge; his faithfulness is a shield and buckler.*" ESV

Confession and Repentance
The Psalms contain suggestions for prayers of confession and repentance, acknowledging human sinfulness and seeking God's grace, forgiveness and mercy. Psalm 51:10, a very well-known psalm, says, "*Create in me a clean heart, O God, and renew a right spirit within me.*" ESV

2. Divine Commands Toward One Another

Justice and Mercy

Several Psalms call for justice and mercy toward the oppressed and vulnerable. For example Psalm 82:3-4 urges, *"Give justice to the weak and the fatherless; maintain the right of the afflicted and the destitute. 4 Rescue the weak and the needy; deliver them from the hand of the wicked."* ESV

Truthfulness and Integrity

The Psalms speak to the importance of truthfulness and integrity in interpersonal relationships. Psalm 15:2-5 says, *"He who walks blamelessly and does what is right and speaks truth in his heart; 3 who does not slander with his tongue and does no evil to his neighbor, nor takes up a reproach against his friend . . . shall never be moved."* ESV

Q15. What does Psalm 133:1 tell us about relationships?

Psalm 133:1 indicates, *"Behold, how good and pleasant it is when brothers dwell in unity!"* ESV

These instructions provide guidance for discipleship, shaping believers' relationship with God, and their interactions with one another. They highlight the importance of praise, trust, confession, unity, justice, mercy, truthfulness, and integrity.

WISDOM LITERATURE – Ecclesiastes

In the book of Ecclesiastes, the emphasis is more on obvious reflections or conclusions rather than specific commands. However, there are still principles that can be drawn from Ecclesiastes regarding how believers are to act toward God and toward one another:

1. Toward God

Fear God and Keep His Commandments

At the end of Ecclesiastes Solomon comes to his conclusion after all has been investigated and examined. He concludes the book with this statement: *"The end of the matter; all has been heard. Fear God and keep his commandments, for this is the whole duty of man."* ESV

Acknowledge God's Sovereignty

There's a continuing theme of recognizing God's sovereignty over all aspects of life, including human endeavors and achievements. Ecclesiastes 3:11 states, *"He has made everything beautiful in its time. Also, he has put eternity into man's heart, yet so that he cannot find out what God has done from the beginning to the end."* ESV

Seek Wisdom

Ecclesiastes encourages the pursuit of wisdom, but it is not a direct command of God. Wisdom and understanding will lead to more knowledge of God, a genuine relationship with God, and a better understanding of His ways. Ecclesiastes 7:12 suggests, *"For the protection of wisdom is like the protection of money, and the advantage of knowledge is that wisdom preserves the life of him who has it."* ESV

2. Toward One Another

Enjoy Relationships

In Ecclesiastes Solomon magnifies the enjoyment of friends and relationships. He says in Ecclesiastes 4:9-10 that, *"Two are better than one, because they have a good reward for their toil. 10 For if they fall, one will lift up his fellow. But woe to him who is alone when he falls and has not another to lift him up!"* ESV

Practice Justice and Equity
While not directly stated in the form of commands, Ecclesiastes reflects on the injustices and inequities in human society and encourages striving for fairness and justice. Ecclesiastes 5:8 observes, *"If you see in a province the oppression of the poor and the violation of justice and righteousness, do not be amazed at the matter, for the high official is watched by a higher, and there are yet higher ones over them."* ESV

Q16. What does Solomon suggest are the virtues in Ecclesiastes 5:18-20? *Behold, what I have seen to be good and fitting is to eat and drink and find enjoyment in all the toil with which one toils under the sun the few days of his life that God has given him, for this is his lot. 19 Everyone also to whom God has given wealth and possessions and power to enjoy them, and to accept his lot and rejoice in his toil—this is the gift of God. 20 For he will not much remember the days of his life because God keeps him occupied with joy in his heart.* ESV

In summary, although Ecclesiastes does not always contain explicit or specific divine commands in the same manner as other books of the Bible, its descriptions of the nature of life, human existence, and the pursuit of meaning in life offer valuable insights into how followers should relate to God and to one another.

3. Solomon's Conclusion: The whole duty of man

Solomon concluded his investigation into the meaning and purpose of life with a significant and profound statement about human duty and destiny. He concludes in Ecclesiastes 12:13: *"The end of the matter; all has been heard. Fear God and keep his commandments, for this is the whole duty of man."* ESV

This conclusion captures the foundation of Solomon's wisdom and provides valuable insights into the meaning, requirements, and implications of living a life of obedience to God.

a. Meaning:

- **Fear God:** The phrase "fear God" does not mean or imply a fearful terror of the Divine. Rather, it means we have a reverential awe and respect for God's righteousness, holiness, sovereignty, power, and majesty. It means we recognize and accept His authority over our life and live in a manner that honors Him.

- **Keep His Commandments:** Keeping God's commandments refers to obeying His laws, instructions, and teachings as revealed throughout Scripture.

b. Requirements:

- **Reverence and Obedience:** The duty of mankind requires both reverence for God and obedience to His commandments. It's not merely about following rules and commands but also about an inward attitude of submission and devotion to God that is the result of true love and submission to His person and authority.

- **Wholehearted Commitment:** Solomon implies that this duty is comprehensive and exhaustive. It demands the entirety of one's being: heart, soul, mind, and strength. He says it is our "whole duty!"

c. Implications:

- **Purpose and Meaning:** Embracing Solomon's conclusion to fear God and keep His commandments provides a sense of purpose and meaning in life. It directs followers and non-followers alike toward fulfilling God's will. This will produce an eternal joy that will overcome the futility ("vanity") described in Ecclesiastes about our earthly existence without God.

- **Guidance for Living:** The "whole duty" serves as a moral and ethical compass in guiding individuals to make the best decisions. It defines what constitutes righteous living and helps provide guidance for daily living.

- **Eternal Significance:** In this conclusion Solomon identifies the eternal significance of human existence. Living in accordance with God's precepts will not only impact one's present life but also his eternal destiny.

Solomon's conclusion identifies the primary focus and ultimate importance of honoring God by living in obedience to His will. It calls for a life characterized by reverence, obedience, and wholehearted devotion to Him.

CONCLUSION

Keeping God's laws and precepts was an absolute requirement of the Law in the Old Testament. But the New Testament also makes some very strong statements about obedience, even though our salvation is not based on works or performance. For example, Paul tells us we are called to obedience:

Romans 1:5-6
Through Christ, God has given us the privilege and authority as apostles to tell Gentiles everywhere what God has done for them, so that they will believe and obey him, bringing glory to his name. 6 And you are included among those Gentiles who have been called to belong to Jesus Christ. NLT

Peter also made it clear that obedience was the expected:

1 Peter 1:2, 14 *according to the foreknowledge of God the Father, in the sanctification of the Spirit, for obedience to Jesus Christ and for sprinkling with his blood: May grace and peace be multiplied to you. . . . 14 As obedient children, do not be conformed to the passions of your former ignorance . . .* ESV

In addition there are some dramatic statements on very important issues that should put obedience at the center of our focus as Jesus followers:

Salvation:
Matthew 19:17 *And he said to him, "Why do you ask me about what is good? There is only one who is good. If you would enter life, keep the commandments."* ESV
Hebrews 5:9 *And being made perfect, he became the source of eternal salvation to all who obey him.* ESV

Knowing Christ:
1 John 2:3-4 *And by this we know that we have come to know him, if we keep his commandments. 4 Whoever says "I know him" but does not keep his commandments is a liar, and the truth is not in him.* ESV

DISSCUSSION QUESTIONS

1. How would you <u>personally</u> summarize the requirements for obedience in this lesson with respect to:

a. Loving God

b. Loving one another

c. Fearing God

d. Keeping His commands, in general

2. How would <u>you</u> personally explain Solomon's conclusion in Ecclesiastes 12:13?

3. How would <u>you</u> answer the question, "Does God really require absolute obedience?"

WHAT I WANT TO REMEMBER

Enter some notes and information that you want to remember about this lesson. It might be a Scripture verse or two, something new you learned, something you want to do, something you want to change, or just something you want to be sure to remember.

Wisdom to Action
Challenge

How can you demonstrate a deeper love and reverence for God through your obedience in a challenging aspect of your life?

Lesson 3
Obedience and Salvation

INTRODUCTION

One of the most frequently discussed issues related to obedience is, "Does God require obedience to attain or maintain salvation?" From a global or broad perspective this is not an easy question to answer. It is much easier to address when we look at specific issues or questions. It is also important to understand what one means by obedience and what particular aspect is in question.

For example, Christianity is not a works-based faith like other religions in the world. All other religions are performance based – the follower must do or perform certain activities or works in order to qualify as a follower or member. That is not the case for Christianity: you simply must have faith in Jesus Christ. You come as you are with all your sins and baggage.

However, there is some level of conformity necessary because the follower has to desire or choose a relationship with Jesus, desire to change their life, and accept Jesus as their Lord and Savior. Therefore, someone might argue that there are requirements. If you do not accept the Gospel and submit your life to Christ, you aren't saved. So, technically there is a level of obedience.

Once an individual is saved, there should be evidence that a conversion actually occurred. There will be evidence such as good works (Ephesians 2:10), fruit of the Spirit

(John 15:8; Galatians 5:22), love for one another (John 13:35), obedience to God's Word (John 8:31), persevering in difficult times (John 8:31-32), and surrendering comforts and taking up your cross (Luke 9:23). These activities can be markers for you to evaluate the status of your faith in your own life. Where do you stand?

Many of the questions that arise and much of the confusion about obedience is the result of the wording of Scripture, because at face value, without understanding the context, it's easy to arrive at wrong conclusions. Note the following:

> **Matthew 19:17** *And he said to him, "Why do you ask me about what is good? There is only one who is good. If you would enter life, keep the commandments."* ESV

> **Hebrews 5:9** *And being made perfect, he became the source of eternal salvation to all who obey him.* ESV

> **1 John 2:3-6** *And by this we know that we have come to know him, if we keep his commandments. 4 Whoever says "I know him" but does not keep his commandments is a liar, and the truth is not in him, 5 but whoever keeps his word, in him truly the love of God is perfected. By this we may be sure that we are in him: 6 whoever says he abides in him ought to walk in the same way in which he walked.* ESV

If these three passages were all you knew or understood, it would be possible to conclude that salvation required obeying a list of commandments.

Q1. What would you personally conclude if you <u>knew only</u> the above?

OBEDIENCE AND SALVATION

Q2. What is required and what is the result for obedience in the following passages?

Philippians 2:14-15
Do all things without grumbling or questioning, 15 that you may be blameless and innocent, children of God without blemish in the midst of a crooked and twisted generation, among whom you shine as lights in the world. ESV

Required:

Result:

Matthew 7:21-23   I Never Knew You
"Not everyone who says to me, 'Lord, Lord,' will enter the kingdom of heaven, but the one who does the will of my Father who is in heaven. 22 On that day many will say to me, 'Lord, Lord, did we not prophesy in your name, and cast out demons in your name, and do many mighty works in your name?' 23 And then will I declare to them, 'I never knew you; depart from me, you workers of lawlessness.'" ESV

Required:

Result:

Romans 2:13 *For it is not the hearers of the law who are righteous before God, but the doers of the law who will be justified.* ESV
Romans 6:16 *Do you not know that if you present yourselves to anyone as obedient slaves, you are slaves of the one whom you obey, either of sin, which leads to death, or of obedience, which leads to righteousness?* ESV
Hebrews 5:9 *And being made perfect, he became the source of eternal salvation to all who obey him,* ESV

Matthew 19:17 *And he said to him, "Why do you ask me about what is good? There is only one who is good. If you would enter life, <u>keep the commandments</u>."* ESV

Required:

Result:

1 John 2:3-6 *And by this we know that we have come to know him, if we <u>keep his commandments</u>. 4 Whoever says "I know him" but does not keep his commandments is a liar, and the truth is not in him, 5 but whoever keeps his word, in him truly the love of God is perfected. By this we may be sure that we are in him: 6 whoever says he abides in him ought to walk in the same way in which he walked.* ESV

Required:

Result:

Mark 10:17-30 The Rich Young Man
*And as he was setting out on his journey, a man ran up and knelt before him and asked him, "Good Teacher, what must I do to inherit eternal life?" 18 And Jesus said to him, "Why do you call me good? No one is good except God alone. 19 You know the commandments: 'Do not murder, Do not commit adultery, Do not steal, Do not bear false witness, Do not defraud, Honor your father and mother.'" 20 And he said to him, "Teacher, all these I have kept from my youth." 21 And Jesus, looking at him, loved him, and said to him, "You lack one thing: go, sell all that you have and give to the poor, and you will have treasure in heaven; and come, follow me." 22 Disheartened by the saying, he went away sorrowful, for he had great possessions.
23 And Jesus looked around and said to his disciples, "How difficult it will be for those who have wealth to enter the kingdom of God!" 24 And the disciples were amazed at his words. But Jesus said to them again, "<u>Children, how difficult it is to enter the kingdom of God!</u> 25 It is easier for a camel to go*

through the eye of a needle than for a rich person to enter the kingdom of God." 26 And they were exceedingly astonished, and said to him, "Then who can be saved?" 27 Jesus looked at them and said, "With man it is impossible, but not with God. For all things are possible with God." 28 Peter began to say to him, "See, we have left everything and followed you." 29 Jesus said, "Truly, I say to you, there is no one who has left house or brothers or sisters or mother or father or children or lands, for my sake and for the gospel, 30 who will not receive a hundredfold now in this time, houses and brothers and sisters and mothers and children and lands, with persecutions, and in the age to come eternal life." ESV

Exhortation:

Required:

Result:

Q3 Conclusion: What do you conclude from the above passages about obedience?

COMMANDS RELATED TO SALVATION

Q4. In the following Scriptures, what do you learn about salvation, faith, or knowing Christ?

Ephesians 2:8-9 *For by grace you have been saved through faith. And this is not your own doing; it is the gift of God, 9 not a result of works, so that no one may boast. ESV*

Luke 14:25-33 The Cost of Discipleship
Now great crowds accompanied him, and he turned and said to them, 26 "If anyone comes to me and does not hate his own father and mother and wife and children and brothers and sisters, yes, and even his own life, he cannot be my disciple. 27 Whoever does not bear his own cross and come after me cannot be my disciple. 28 For which of you, desiring to build a tower, does not first sit down and count the cost, whether he has enough to complete it? . . . 33 So therefore, any one of you who does not renounce all that he has cannot be my disciple." ESV
[NOTE: The meaning of "hate" in this passage is not what we might think. It's a comparative word meaning "love less."]

Acts 2:38 *And Peter said to them, "Repent and be baptized every one of you in the name of Jesus Christ for the forgiveness of your sins, and you will receive the gift of the Holy Spirit." ESV*

Romans 10:9-10 *because, if you confess with your mouth that Jesus is Lord and believe in your heart that God raised him from the dead, you will be saved. 10 For with the heart one believes and is justified, and with the mouth one confesses and is saved. ESV*

Mark 16:16 *Whoever believes and is baptized will be saved, but whoever does not believe will be condemned.* ESV

1 John 2:3-6 *And by this we know that we have come to know him, if we keep his commandments. 4 Whoever says "I know him" but does not keep his commandments is a liar, and the truth is not in him, 5 but whoever keeps his word, in him truly the love of God is perfected. By this we may be sure that we are in him: 6 whoever says he abides in him ought to walk in the same way in which he walked.* ESV

OBEDIENCE AND SALVATION

It is obvious from the above that the relationship between obedience and salvation might be a bit cloudy. This issue can be subtle and even confusing. It is certainly multifaceted. While the New Testament clearly indicates that salvation is received by grace through faith in Jesus Christ apart from works (Ephesians 2:8-9), it also stresses the importance of obedience as *evidence* of genuine faith and having a relationship with Jesus/God. Confusion can arise over the question of which comes first.

Following are key points regarding disobedience and salvation in the New Testament.

Q5. What do you learn about <u>salvation</u> in the following Scriptures?

John 3:16 *For God so loved the world, that he gave his only Son, that whoever believes in him should not perish but have eternal life.* ESV

Romans 10:9 *because, if you confess with your mouth that Jesus is Lord and believe in your heart that God raised him from the dead, you will be saved.* ESV

Titus 3:5 *he saved us, not because of works done by us in righteousness, but according to his own mercy, by the washing of regeneration and renewal of the Holy Spirit,* ESV

Q6. What do we learn about <u>faith</u> and salvation in the following?

James 2:17 *So also faith by itself, if it does not have works, is dead.* ESV

Q7. What do we learn about <u>perseverance</u> and faith in the following?

Matthew 24:13 *But the one who endures to the end will be saved.* ESV

Hebrews 10:36 *For you have need of endurance, so that when you have done the will of God you may receive what is promised.* ESV

Q8. What if we fail and commit sin?

1 John 1:9 *If we confess our sins, he is faithful and just to forgive us our sins and to cleanse us from all unrighteousness.* ESV

While obedience is not a prerequisite for salvation, it is an important aspect of the continuing Christian life and serves as evidence of genuine faith and a true relationship with God/Jesus. Believers are called to persevere in faith and obedience, guarding against apostasy and to repent of sin when necessary. Salvation is ultimately a work of God's grace, received by faith, but it is evidenced by a life of obedience and devotion to God.

SUMMARY

The Bible never explicitly states that "obedience" is a requirement for salvation in the sense that it says directly that one must obey God's commands in order to "earn" salvation. Instead, the Bible teaches that salvation is received by grace through faith in Jesus Christ. The New Testament consistently emphasizes that salvation is a gift of God's grace, freely offered to all who believe and accept Jesus Christ as Lord and Savior. The primary requirement for salvation is faith in Jesus Christ. John 3:16 famously declares if you believe in Christ you shall not perish but have eternal life. Similarly, Romans 10:9 teaches that if you confess with your mouth that Jesus is Lord and believe in your heart that God raised him from the dead, you will be saved.

Jesus taught that those who love Him will obey His commands (John 14:15), and James emphasized that faith without works is dead (James 2:17).

The clear message is that genuine faith produces a transformed life characterized by obedience to God's will and commands. Jesus does call His followers to a life of discipleship and obedience. He instructs His disciples to take up their cross and follow Him (Matthew 16:24), which means obeying His teachings and following His ways.

Salvation, on the other hand is a one-time event. Although it is a past event it is a continuing reality toward a future eternity.

> **Philippians 2:12-13** *Therefore, my beloved, as you have always obeyed, so now, not only as in my presence but much more in my absence, <u>work out your own salvation</u> with fear and trembling, 13 for it is God who works in you, both to will and to work for his good pleasure.* ESV

While obedience is not the mechanism for initial salvation, it is an important if not essential aspect of the Faith.

CAN YOU LOSE YOUR SALVATION?

The concept of whether one can lose their salvation is a historical topic of theological debate among Christians. There are reasonable arguments on both sides of the issue because different theological traditions interpret Scripture differently on this matter. Some believe in the doctrine of "eternal security" or "once saved, always saved." If this is your belief then those who genuinely trust in Christ for salvation cannot lose their salvation because God will hold them fast to the end, this they will not turn away. Others believe that it is possible for a believer to fall away from faith and reject their salvation.

Scripture contains passages that seem to suggest both perspectives, and the interpretation of these passages varies among respected Christians. Here are several key passages that are frequently cited in discussions about the possibility of losing salvation due to apostasy, disobedience, or sin.

Hebrews 6:4-6
This passage warns about the danger of falling away from the faith after experiencing the benefits of being part of the Christian community. It describes those who have been enlightened, tasted the heavenly gift, shared in the Holy Spirit, and tasted the goodness of the Word of God, yet have fallen away. It says that it is impossible to restore them again to repentance, suggesting severe consequences for apostasy.

Hebrews 10:26-31
This passage warns about the severe judgment that awaits those who persist in willful sinning after knowing the truth. It describes an expectation of judgment and raging fire that will consume the enemies of God. It sounds like eternal hell!

The New Testament also issues warnings against falling away from the faith and returning to a life of disobedience or unbelief. These following passages warn about the danger of apostasy and the severe consequences for those who persist in willful sinning and rejecting the gospel.

2 Peter 2:20-22
Peter describes the danger of returning to a life of sin and disobedience after having escaped the evil of the world through the knowledge of Christ. He compares such people to dogs returning to their vomit or pigs returning to wallow in the mud, suggesting a grievous outcome for those who turn away from the faith or reject Christ.

Matthew 7:21-23
Jesus warns about the danger of professing faith but not living in obedience to God's will. He states that not everyone who calls Him "Lord" will enter the kingdom of heaven, but only those who do the will of God the Father. Jesus tells the listeners, "I never knew you; depart from me."

While the passages above paint a very serious picture, there are other passages that emphasize the security of believers in Christ and the assurance of their salvation.

Q9. What assurance do we receive in the following verses?

John 10:27-29 *My sheep hear my voice, and I know them, and they follow me. 28 I give them eternal life, and they will never perish, and no one will snatch them out of my hand. 29 My Father, who has given them to me, is greater than all, and no one is able to snatch them out of the Father's hand.* ESV

Romans 8:38-39 *For I am sure that neither death nor life, nor angels nor rulers, nor things present nor things to come, nor powers, 39 nor height nor depth, nor anything else in all creation, will be able to separate us from the love of God in Christ Jesus our Lord.* ESV

The answer to the question of whether one can lose their salvation for sin and disobedience is a matter of religious interpretation and debate. Christians hold differing views on this topic based on their interpretation of Scripture and theological tradition. However, both sides would call you to live a life of obedience as a demonstration of the genuineness of your faith

CONSEQUENCES

The primary focus of the New Testament is on God's grace, forgiveness, and salvation through Jesus Christ. It does, however, warn the reader of the consequences of persisting in disobedience and rejecting the gospel. Here are some key examples regarding the punishment or judgment for disobedience in the New Testament:

Separation For Not Knowing God
2 Thessalonians 1:9 *They* [those who do not know God] *will suffer the punishment of eternal destruction, away from the presence of the Lord and from the glory of his might . . .* ESV

Consequences of Sin
Romans 6:23 *For the wages of sin is death, but the free gift of God is eternal life in Christ Jesus our Lord.* ESV

Judgment and Wrath For Hardened Hearts
Romans 2:5 *But because of your hard and impenitent heart you are storing up wrath for yourself on the day of wrath when God's righteous judgment will be revealed.* ESV

Eternal Punishment For Lack of Compassion
Matthew 25:46 *And these* [those who show no compassion to Jesus' followers and thus demonstrate they have no devotion to Him] *will go away into eternal punishment, but the righteous into eternal life.* ESV

All Will be Judged
2 Corinthians 5:10 *For we must all appear before the judgment seat of Christ, so that each one may receive what is due for what he has done in the body, whether good or evil.* ESV

Exclusion From the Kingdom For the Unrighteous
1 Corinthians 6:9-10 *Do you not know that the unrighteous will not inherit the kingdom of God? Do not be deceived: neither the sexually immoral, nor idolaters, nor adulterers, nor men who practice homosexuality, 10 nor thieves, nor the greedy, nor drunkards, nor revilers, nor swindlers will inherit the kingdom of God.* ESV

While the New Testament describes abundant grace and forgiveness through Jesus Christ, it also describes the seriousness of disobedience and the consequences of rejecting God's offer of salvation. Believers are urged to heed the warnings, repent of sin, and turn to God in faith and obedience, knowing that judgment awaits those who reject God.

WHAT DO I WANT TO REMEMBER?

Enter some notes and information that you want to remember about this lesson. It might be a Scripture verse or two, something new you learned, something you want to do, something you want to change, or just something you want to be sure to remember.

Wisdom to Action
Challenge

Reflect on your motivations for obedience. How can you shift your focus from earning God's favor to expressing love and gratitude for your salvation?

Lesson 4
Punishment For Disobedience

Scripture has a great deal more to say about punishment for disobedience to the laws, teachings, and commands of God. We will generally not discuss the issue of loss of salvation in this material, as it was examined in the previous lesson.

TESTING

It is important to know up front that God may test you so you will recognize your own strengths and weaknesses. God already knows how you will respond, but He may want *you* to know. Let's examine the experiences of some notable characters in the Bible.

Job

Satan challenged God regarding the integrity of Job's faith. God allowed Satan to test Job by giving him various trials, including the loss of his wealth, family, and health. Job remained faithful throughout the ordeal. (Job 1-2)

Abraham

God tested Abraham by asking him to sacrifice his son, Isaac, as a burnt offering. Abraham demonstrated his obedience by preparing to carry out the command, but God intervened and provided a ram substitute sacrifice.

Genesis 22:1, 12, 18 *Sometime later God <u>tested</u> Abraham. He said to him, "Abraham!" "Here I am," he replied. . . . 12 "Do not lay a hand on the boy," he said. "Do not do anything to him. Now I know that you <u>fear God</u>, because you have not withheld from me your son, your only son . . . 18 and through your offspring all nations on earth will be blessed, because you have <u>obeyed me</u>."* NIV

Noah

Hebrews 11:7 *By faith Noah, when warned about things not yet seen, in holy fear built an ark to save his family. By his faith he condemned the world and became heir of the righteousness that comes by faith.* NIV

One might consider the story of Noah as a form of testing, particularly in terms of Noah's obedience and faithfulness to God's commands amidst a corrupt and sinful world. In Genesis 6-9, God chose to spare Noah and his family, instructing him to build an ark to save himself, his family, and every kind of animal. This command placed a significant burden on Noah, requiring him to commit to a lengthy and challenging task in the face of skepticism and ridicule from his peers and neighbors. Noah spent nearly 100 years building the ark.

Noah's obedience and perseverance can be seen as a test of his faith and devotion to God amidst a world filled with corruption and disobedience.

Daniel and his Friends

FOOD: Daniel and his friends were tested when they were taken into captivity in Babylon and offered the king's food and wine. They chose to remain obedient to their dietary laws and God's commands, requesting a diet of vegetables and water. (Daniel 1:8ff)

LIONS' DEN: Evil men around King Darius forced Daniel to declare he would not stop praying to his God and certainly not pray to King Darius as a god. The penalty was being thrown into the lions' den, where Daniel was ultimately protected by God. The king was overjoyed and removed Daniel from the den, while those who falsely accused Daniel were crushed by the lions. (Daniel 6)

Jesus

After his baptism, Jesus was led by the Spirit into the wilderness to be tempted by the devil. He was tested three times, but He remained obedient to God's will, resisting temptation by quoting Scripture. (Matthew 4:1-11)

These examples illustrate how God tested individuals and groups in Scripture to evaluate their obedience, faithfulness, and commitment to His commands. The inherent reason for any testing from God is to see how we react – do we respond according to God's commands, laws, and teachings? Or do we think we know more than God, and decide we will not follow the rules? Rebellion against God is the basic definition of sin.

Rebellion can be tested individually or it can apply to a nation. Israel was tested in that manner.

Israel

> *I will use them* [other nations] *to test Israel and see whether they will keep the way of the LORD and walk in it as their forefathers did.* (Judges 2:22 NIV)

God tested the obedience of the Israelites by giving them the Ten Commandments and other laws at Mount Sinai (Exodus 19-20). He instructed Moses to convey these commandments to the people, in order to determine if they would obey His covenant.

PUNISHMENT FOR DISOBEDIENCE

The New Testament identifies forms of punishment or disciplinary measures for believers who persist in disobedience or rebellion against God. While these consequences are distinct from eternal judgment, they serve as corrective measures intended to bring believers back into obedience with God's will and purposes.

Q1. What do we learn about punishment in the following New Testament Scriptures?

2 Thessalonians 1:8 *He will punish those who do not know God and do not obey the gospel of our Lord Jesus.* NIV

Ephesians 5:6 *Let no one deceive you with empty words, for because of such things God's wrath comes on those who are disobedient.* NIV

1 Peter 4:17 *For it is time for judgment to begin with the family of God; and if it begins with us, what will the outcome be for those who do not obey the gospel of God?* NIV

2 Corinthians 10:5-6 *We demolish arguments and every pretension that sets itself up against the knowledge of God, and we take captive every thought to make it obedient to Christ. 6 And we will be ready to punish every act of disobedience, once your obedience is complete.* NIV

Q2. What is the offense and the resulting punishment in the following Scriptures?

Hebrews 12:5-11
And have you forgotten the exhortation that addresses you as sons? "My son, do not regard lightly the discipline of the Lord, nor be weary when reproved by him. 6 For the Lord disciplines the one he loves, and chastises every son whom he receives." 7 It is for discipline that you have to endure. God is treating you as sons. For what son is there whom his father does not discipline? 8 If you are left without discipline, in which all have participated, then you are illegitimate children and not sons. 9 Besides this, we have had earthly fathers who disciplined us and we respected them. Shall we not much more be subject to the Father of spirits and live? 10 For they disciplined us for a short time as it seemed best to them, but he disciplines us for our good, that we may share his holiness. 11 For the moment all discipline seems painful rather than pleasant, but later it yields the peaceful fruit of righteousness to those who have been trained by it. ESV

1 Corinthians 3:12-15
Now if anyone builds on the foundation with gold, silver, precious stones, wood, hay, straw — *each one's work will become manifest, for the Day will disclose it, because it will be revealed by fire, and the fire will test what sort of work each one has done. 14 If the work that anyone has built on the foundation survives, he will receive a reward. 15 If anyone's work is burned up, he will suffer loss, though he himself will be saved, but only as through fire.* ESV

1 Corinthians 11:29-30
For anyone who eats and drinks without discerning the body eats and drinks judgment on himself. 30 That is why many of you are weak and ill, and some have died. ESV

Galatians 6:1
Brothers, if anyone is caught in any transgression, you who are spiritual should restore him in a spirit of gentleness. Keep watch on yourself, lest you too be tempted. ESV

Matthew 18:15-17
If your brother sins against you, go and tell him his fault, between you and him alone. If he listens to you, you have gained your brother. 16 But if he does not listen, take one or two others along with you, that every charge may be established by the evidence of two or three witnesses. 17 If he refuses to listen to them, tell it to the church. And if he refuses to listen even to the church, let him be to you as a Gentile and a tax collector. ESV

The examples of punishment above were designed to bring about repentance, restoration, and spiritual growth in the lives of believers. While they involve some form of punishment, they ultimately produce better disciples, intending to lead them to greater obedience and conformity to the righteous of Christ. They might be thought of as "correction" more than punishment.

Q3. What do we learn from the following about obedience and specific kinds of sinful situations?

Continuing Sin
Romans 6:1-2 *What shall we say then? Are we to continue in sin that grace may abound? 2 By no means! How can we who died to sin still live in it?* ESV

Sins of the Flesh
Galatians 5:19-21 *Now the works of the flesh are evident: sexual immorality, impurity, sensuality, 20 idolatry, sorcery, enmity, strife, jealousy, fits of anger, rivalries, dissensions, divisions, 21 envy, drunkenness, orgies, and things like these. I warn you, as I warned you before, that those who do such things will not inherit the kingdom of God.* ESV

Sexual Immorality and Idolatry
Ephesians 5:5-6 *For you may be sure of this, that everyone who is sexually immoral or impure, or who is covetous (that is, an idolater), has no inheritance in the kingdom of Christ and God. 6 Let no one deceive you with empty words, for because of these things the wrath of God comes upon the sons of disobedience.* ESV
Colossians 3:5-6 *Put to death therefore what is earthly in you: sexual immorality, impurity, passion, evil desire, and covetousness, which is idolatry. 6 On account of these the wrath of God is coming.* ESV

Intentional Sin

Hebrews 10:26-31 *For if we go on sinning deliberately after receiving the knowledge of the truth, there no longer remains a sacrifice for sins, 27 but a fearful expectation of judgment, and a fury of fire that will consume the adversaries. 28 Anyone who has set aside the law of Moses dies without mercy on the evidence of two or three witnesses. 29 How much worse punishment, do you think, will be deserved by the one who has spurned the Son of God, and has profaned the blood of the covenant by which he was sanctified, and has outraged the Spirit of grace? 30 For we know him who said, "Vengeance is mine; I will repay." And again, "The Lord will judge his people." 31 It is a fearful thing to fall into the hands of the living God.* ESV

James 4:17 *So whoever knows the right thing to do and fails to do it, for him it is sin.* ESV

Backsliding

2 Peter 2:20-22 *For if, after they have escaped the defilements of the world through the knowledge of our Lord and Savior Jesus Christ, they are again entangled in them and overcome, the last state has become worse for them than the first. 21 For it would have been better for them never to have known the way of righteousness than after knowing it to turn back from the holy commandment delivered to them. 22 What the true proverb says has happened to them: "The dog returns to its own vomit, and the sow, after washing herself, returns to wallow in the mire."* ESV

These Scriptures describe the serious consequences of living in disobedience or persisting in a pattern of sin, particularly for believers. Continuing and persistent disobedience not only jeopardizes one's relationship with God but also carries the risk of facing divine judgment. Therefore, we should pursue lives characterized by obedience to God's commands, empowered by the Holy Spirit, and rooted solidly in the gospel.

MORE SERIOUS WARNINGS

One might think that the above pretty well covers the subject of serious sin and punishment. But there are several other important warnings and teachings in the New Testament regarding the consequences of disobedience that we should not overlook. What do you learn in the following passages?

I Never Knew You
Matthew 7:21-23 *Not everyone who says to me, 'Lord, Lord,' will enter the kingdom of heaven, but the one who does the will of my Father who is in heaven. 22 On that day many will say to me, 'Lord, Lord, did we not prophesy in your name, and cast out demons in your name, and do many mighty works in your name?' 23 And then will I declare to them, 'I never knew you; depart from me, you workers of lawlessness.'* ESV

Rejection of the Faith

1 Timothy 4:1-2 *Now the Spirit expressly says that in later times some will depart from the faith by devoting themselves to deceitful spirits and teachings of demons, 2 through the insincerity of liars whose consciences are seared,* ESV

Idolatry

1 Corinthians 10:7-12 *Do not be idolaters as some of them were; as it is written, "The people sat down to eat and drink and rose up to play." 8 We must not indulge in sexual immorality as some of them did, and twenty-three thousand fell in a single day. 9 We must not put Christ to the test, as some of them did and were destroyed by serpents, 10 nor grumble, as some of them did and were destroyed by the Destroyer. 11 Now these things happened to them as an example, but they were written down for our instruction, on whom the end of the ages has come. 12 Therefore let anyone who thinks that he stands take heed lest he fall.* ESV

Obedience is the Proof

1 John 2:3-6 *And by this we know that we have come to know him, if we keep his commandments. 4 Whoever says "I know him" but does not keep his commandments is a liar, and the truth is not in him, 5 but whoever keeps his word, in him truly the love of God is perfected. By this we may be sure that we are in him: 6 whoever says he abides in him ought to walk in the same way in which he walked.* ESV

All these warnings highlight and confirm the seriousness of disobedience and the importance of obeying God's commands. They should remind us of our need to remain vigilant and guard against deception and false teachings. We are told throughout Scripture to stand fast in our faith, living lives characterized by obedience, righteousness, and devotion to God.

CONCLUSION

Our hope and prayer is that you realize the seriousness of sin. God hates sin. And things that are sinful or corrupt cannot exist permanently in the presence of a holy and righteous God. That includes you and me!

Jesus told the crowd in Luke 12 to beware of religious hypocrisy. He said, "*I tell you, my friends, do not fear those who kill the body, and after that have nothing more that they can do. 5 But I will warn you whom to fear: fear him who, after he has killed, has authority to cast into hell. Yes, I tell you, fear him!*" (Luke 12:4-5 ESV) [Jesus is talking here about real terror; this is not a reference to the "fear of the Lord."]

Jesus then followed this up by saying something that none of us should forget:

> "And I tell you, everyone who acknowledges me before men, the Son of Man also will acknowledge before the angels of God, 9 but the one who denies me before men will be denied before the angels of God. 10 And everyone who speaks a word against the Son of Man will be forgiven, but the one who blasphemes against the Holy Spirit will not be forgiven. (Lk 12:8-10 ESV)

WHAT I WANT TO REMEMBER

Enter some notes and information that you want to remember about this lesson. It might be a Scripture verse or two, something new you learned, something you want to do, something you want to change, or just something you want to be sure to remember.

Wisdom to Action
Challenge

What area of persistent disobedience might God be revealing in your life? What steps will you take towards repentance and spiritual growth in this area?

Lesson 5
The Need for Christ

*And this is love, that we walk according
to his commandments; this is the commandment,
just as you have heard from the beginning,
so that you should walk in it.*
2 John 6 ESV

LOVING CHRIST

Obedience results from loving Jesus. If we have accepted
Jesus as Savior and Lord, being a follower or disciple
means that we will have a growing love relationship with
the Son of God.

Loving Christ means we have a deep devotion that results
from choice rather than emotion. It is selfless and it is the
highest form of love, characterized by sacrificial giving,
commitment, and obedience to the one who made eternal
life possible for us by paying our sin debt. Loving Christ
with *agape* means being willing to sacrifice our own
desires, ambitions, and comforts in order to honor Him
and serve His purposes.

Agape love is marked by unwavering commitment and
loyalty. Loving Christ with agape requires selfless devotion,
obeying His teachings, and living in accordance with His
teachings and precepts. This level of trust and obedience
may require perseverance through difficulties, challenges,
and trials.

It also means seeking His will, His glory, and the advancement of His Kingdom above personal agendas or ambitions. It includes humility and a willingness to surrender control of our lives to Him and His plans for us.

Loving Christ means we love others as indicated in the second half of the Great Commandment. We are to love others like ourselves, showing kindness to those in need in order to reflect His love to the world. It is an active love because it means actively serving Him by serving others, sharing the message of His love and salvation to the world.

In summary, it means we are fully committed to His purposes, prioritizing His commands, and follow His teaching above all else. It is a transformative love relationship that dictates every aspect of our lives, reflecting the profound depth of His love for us.

THE NECESSITY OF CHRIST

Our obedience comes from loving Christ and being committed to following Him. John states very clearly the relationship between loving Christ and obedience:

> **John 14:15** *If you love me, you will obey what I command.* NIV
> **2 John 6** *And this is love: that we walk in obedience to his commands. As you have heard from the beginning, his command is that you walk in love.* NIV

Q1. What do we learn about this love relationship from the following passages?
1 John 5:3 *This is love for God: to obey his commands. And his commands are not burdensome.* NIV

John 15:10 *If you obey my commands, you will remain in my love, just as I have obeyed my Father's commands and remain in his love.* NIV

Galatians 2:16-21 . . . *no one will ever be saved by obeying the law* . . . (NLT)

The passage from Galatians reminds us that obedience to religious laws can never save us. But when we accept Christ, we are increasingly motivated to obey God out of love for him.

Q2. Why do we need Jesus?

Explaining the need for Christ in relation to obedience requires we understand the role of Jesus in accomplishing the restoration and reconciliation of God's people. The Bible is a story of how God pursues man in order to reconcile humanity to Himself. If such pursuit was left to man, no one would ever be saved because man would ultimately choose self over God. Jesus is God's solution for our sin problem.

What are the reasons we need Jesus in the following passages?

Romans 3:23 *for all have sinned and fall short of the glory of God,* ESV

Ephesians 2:8-9 *For by grace you have been saved through faith. And this is not your own doing; it is the gift of God, 9 not a result of works, so that no one may boast.* ESV

Matthew 5:17 *Do not think that I have come to abolish the Law or the Prophets; I have not come to abolish them but to fulfill them.* ESV

1 Peter 2:24 *He himself bore our sins in his body on the tree, that we might die to sin and live to righteousness. By his wounds you have been healed.* ESV

Galatians 5:22-23 *But the fruit of the Spirit is love, joy, peace, patience, kindness, goodness, faithfulness, 23 gentleness, self-control; against such things there is no law.* ESV

The need for Jesus arises because of our inability to save ourselves from sin and our inability to fulfill the demands of God's law. God requires perfection and we do not have the ability to meet that standard.

Jesus fulfills the law on our behalf, atones for our sin through His shedding of blood on the Cross, and provides the basis for our salvation by grace through faith. Through faith in Christ, believers are empowered to live obedient lives and experience reconciliation with God.

HOLY SPIRIT

The third member of the Trinity, the Holy Spirit, plays a crucial role in enabling believers to achieve obedience to God's teaching. He is the power that believers can call on to be obedient.

Q3. What are the ways in the following passages that identify ways in which the Holy Spirit facilitates obedience?

Ephesians 1:13-14 *In him you also, when you heard the word of truth, the gospel of your salvation, and believed in him, were sealed with the promised Holy Spirit, 14 who is the guarantee of our inheritance until we acquire possession of it, to the praise of his glory.* ESV

John 16:13 *When the Spirit of truth comes, he will guide you into all the truth, for he will not speak on his own authority, but whatever he hears he will speak, and he will declare to you the things that are to come.* ESV

John 16:8 *And when he comes, he will convict the world concerning sin and righteousness and judgment:* ESV

Titus 3:5 *He saved us, not because of works done by us in righteousness, but according to his own mercy, by the washing of regeneration and renewal of the Holy Spirit,* ESV

Romans 12:2 *Do not be conformed to this world, but be transformed by the renewal of your mind, that by testing you may discern what is the will of God, what is good and acceptable and perfect.* ESV

1 Corinthians 2:12-13 *Now we have received not the spirit of the world, but the Spirit who is from God, that we might understand the things freely given us by God. 13 And we impart this in words not taught by human wisdom but taught by the Spirit, interpreting spiritual truths to those who are spiritual.* ESV

Acts 1:8 *But you will receive power when the Holy Spirit has come upon you, and you will be my witnesses in Jerusalem and in all Judea and Samaria, and to the end of the earth."* ESV

Romans 8:26-27 *Likewise the Spirit helps us in our weakness. For we do not know what to pray for as we ought, but the Spirit himself intercedes for us with groanings too deep for words. 27 And he who searches hearts knows what is the mind of the Spirit, because the Spirit intercedes for the saints according to the will of God.* ESV

In summary, the Holy Spirit is intimately involved in the process of enabling believers to achieve obedience to God. The Holy Spirit produces fruit in the lives of believers, including love, joy, peace, patience, kindness, goodness, faithfulness, gentleness, and self-control (Galatians 5:22-23). These qualities enable believers to live obediently and reflect the character of Christ.

By convicting individuals of sin, regenerating hearts, indwelling believers, providing guidance, empowering for service, and interceding for believers, the Holy Spirit empowers believers to live obedient lives in accordance with God's will and purpose for them.

DISCUSSION QUESTIONS?

1. Do you think you can love God and not keep all the commandments? Explain.

2. Which of the commands in the Bible relative to your obedience do you think are the most important? Why?

3. Do you think it is possible to live a life acceptable to God without keeping every little command? Why? Why not?

4. How important is the Holy Spirit in your life? Do you think He is necessary to live a life acceptable to God? Explain.

5. In your own words how would you explain the need for God's help to live in conformity with the "requirements" of the Christian faith?

6. Matthew 5:48 says, "*You therefore must be perfect, as your heavenly Father is perfect.*" If this verse is literally true, how can anyone be found acceptable to God?

WHAT I WANT TO REMEMBER

Enter some notes and information that you want to remember about this lesson. It might be a Scripture verse or two, something new you learned, something you want to do, something you want to change, or just something you want to be sure to remember.

Wisdom to Action
Challenge

How can you deepen your love relationship with Jesus this week? What specific act of obedience will demonstrate your growing commitment to Him?

Lesson 6
The Fear Of The Lord

"The fear of the Lord" is a phrase found frequently in the Old Testament, especially in the wisdom literature like Psalms, Proverbs, and Ecclesiastes, but it is used throughout the entire Bible. Understanding its meaning requires context from the cultural and theological framework of ancient Israel.

In this lesson we will be looking at how the fear of the Lord relates to obedience.

MEANING IN OLD TESTAMENT

Reverential Awe
The fundamental meaning of this term might be described by the concept of reverent awe. In the Old Testament, "fear of the Lord" frequently denotes a reverential awe and respect for God's holiness, power, and sovereignty. It acknowledges God's supreme authority over all creation and recognizes His right to judge and discipline. It does not necessarily mean that we are to be afraid or be in terror of God. But, there is a hint that anyone who stands in the presence or mercy of God has reason to be overwhelmed and some knee-shaking would not be out of line.

In terms of an official definition we would describe the "fear of the Lord" as:

> The *fear of the Lord* encompasses dreading
> God's displeasure, desiring His favor, revering
> His holiness, submitting cheerfully to His will,
> being grateful for His benefits, sincerely
> worshipping Him, and conscientiously
> obeying His commandments.

Fear in this context is the reverent regard for God, accompanied by awe and fear of punishment for disobedience. It might be described as reverent trepidation – a healthy or holy fear. It is reverence or respect, which has its foundation in love and causes one to endeavor to please God rather than offend Him. This attitude gives God the place of glory, honor, reverence, worship, and pre-eminence He deserves.

Wisdom and Understanding

The fear of the Lord is also closely associated with wisdom and understanding. Proverbs 9:10 states, "*The fear of the Lord is the beginning of wisdom, and knowledge of the Holy One is insight.*" (ESV) This is intended to mean that true wisdom starts with a proper reverence for and understanding of the laws of God. God's ways must be the foundation of knowledge and understanding or our resulting words and actions will not be properly based in truth and reality, even though we may think they are.

Turning from Evil

The fear of the Lord also involves turning away from evil and wickedness. Proverbs 3:7 advises, "*Do not be wise in your own eyes; fear the Lord and turn away from evil.*" (ESV) It requires living a life that aligns with God's moral and ethical standards or principles. It includes recognition that God is the underlying source of understanding and wisdom and not self. Therefore we must rely on God's moral standards not those of man.

Blessings and Protection

The Old Testament often associates the fear of the Lord with blessings, protection, and long life. For example Psalm 34:7-9 declares, *The angel of the Lord encamps around those who fear him, and delivers them. 8 Oh, taste and see that the Lord is good! Blessed is the man who takes refuge in him! 9 Oh, fear the Lord, you his saints, for those who fear him have no lack!* ESV

MEANING TODAY

Today the fear of the Lord involves maintaining a reverential awe and submission to God's authority. We surrender to Him as Creator, Healer, and Savior. It means acknowledging God's supremacy in our lives and yielding to His will. It recognizes His sovereignty and the almighty power and wisdom that make up His presence.

The Bible indicates the importance of seeking and acting according to the will of God: In the Lord's Prayer (Matthew 6:10) it says "*Your kingdom come, your will be done, on earth as it is in heaven.*" (ESV) Jesus teaches His disciples to pray for God's will to be done on earth. This indicates the importance of aligning our desires and actions with the will of God.

Romans 12:2 indicates, "*Do not be conformed to this world, but be transformed by the renewal of your mind, that by testing you may discern what is the will of God, what is good and acceptable and perfect.*" (ESV) This verse emphasizes the need for followers to be transformed in their thinking and of discerning God's will. By renewing our minds through Scripture and prayer, we can better understand and align ourselves with God's purposes.

Like in the Old Testament, the "fear of the Lord" is linked to wisdom and understanding for believers today. It implies seeking God's guidance and aligning one's life with

His truth and principles as revealed in Scripture. Solomon's conclusion in Ecclesiastes 12:13 is as true today as it was when he concluded that we should *"Fear God and keep his commandments, for this is the whole duty of man."*

The fear of the Lord teaches and motivates believers to live righteously and avoid sin. It prompts individuals to make choices that honor God and reflect His character in their thoughts, words, and actions. In the New Testament Jesus is our righteousness and it is His pure and blameless life that was sacrificed for our benefit.

Q1. What do the following passages tell us about living righteously?

Matthew 5:20: *For I tell you that unless your righteousness surpasses that of the Pharisees and the teachers of the law, you will certainly not enter the kingdom of heaven.* NIV

Romans 6:13: *Do not offer any part of yourself to sin as an instrument of wickedness, but rather offer yourselves to God as those who have been brought from death to life; and offer every part of yourself to him as an instrument of righteousness.* NIV

Ephesians 4:24: *and to put on the new self, created to be like God in true righteousness and holiness.* NIV

These verses highlight the importance of followers of Jesus living righteously as a result of their faith and relationship with God. Living righteously involves walking in step with the Holy Spirit, allowing His guidance and power to lead us away from sinful desires and toward a life characterized by the fruit of the Spirit.

In 1 Peter 1:15-16 Peter calls followers to holy living and says that those called are to be holy as God is holy. Peter exhorts believers to live holy lives, reflecting the character of God who has called them. This includes living righteously in all aspects of life so that we can ultimately be presented to God as blameless through Christ.

The fear of the Lord continues to be associated with blessings and spiritual protection for followers today. It leads to a deeper intimacy with God and opens the door to experiencing His favor and provision in life.

FEAR OF THE LORD and OBEDIENCE – Comparisons

The two conclusions of Solomon relative to the fear of the Lord and in keeping God's commands are closely related but distinct aspects of biblical teaching. They each emphasize different aspects of the believer's relationship with God.

The fear of the Lord can be seen as the foundational attitude that motivates obedience to God's commands. When individuals fear the Lord (reverence His holiness, acknowledge His authority, and recognize His sovereignty) they are more inclined to obey His commandments because of their reverence, love, or respect.

Keeping His commands is the practical result of the fear of the Lord. It provides the inherent guidance and direction for understanding and following God's will. It serves as the internal compass that steers believers to obey.

"The fear of the Lord" focuses on the inward attitude of reverential awe toward God, whereas keeping God's commands involves outward actions of obedience and adherence to His specific instructions. Our faith is often seen as the starting point or foundation of wisdom and obedience, while keeping God's commands represents the practical application of that faith in everyday life.

While the fear of the Lord encompasses the orientation of the heart toward God, keeping God's commands deals with the behavioral aspect of following His will. Both are interconnected. The fear of the Lord influences one's obedience which deepens one's reverence for God. They are complementary aspects of the believer's relationship with God. Fear provides the spiritual disposition that fuels obedience, while obedience to God's commands demonstrates and reinforces the fear of the Lord.

Q2. What do you learn about obedience linked to the fear of the Lord in the following passages?
Deuteronomy 6:2 . . . *so that you, your children and their children after them may <u>fear the LORD</u> your God as long as you live by keeping all his decrees and commands that I give you, and so that you may enjoy long life.* NIV

Deuteronomy 10:12-13 *And now, O Israel, what does the LORD your God ask of you but to fear the LORD your God, to walk in all his ways, to love him, to serve the LORD your God with all your heart and with all your soul, and to observe the LORD's commands and decrees that I am giving you today for your own good?* NIV

Psalms 128:1 *Blessed are all who fear the LORD, who walk in his ways.* NIV

Psalms 111:10 *The fear of the LORD is the beginning of wisdom; all who follow his precepts have good understanding . . .* NIV

Psalms 103:17-18 (NIV) *But from everlasting to everlasting the LORD's love is with those who fear him, and his righteousness with their children's children – with those who keep his covenant and remember to obey his precepts.*

DISCUSSION QUESTIONS

1. What do you think Solomon meant by "whole duty of man" in Ecclesiastes 12:13, relative to the fear of the Lord?

2. How would <u>you</u> relate Solomon's conclusion to fear God (Ecclesiastes 12:13) to the second conclusion to obey His commands?

3. What will happen if we don't fear God pursuant to Ecclesiastes 12:14, which says, "*For God will bring every deed into judgment, with every secret thing, whether good or evil.*" ESV

4. Do you think people in the church today "fear God?" Why? Why not?

5. Do you think people outside the church fear God? Should they?

WHAT I WANT TO REMEMBER

Enter some notes and information that you want to remember about this lesson. It might be a Scripture verse or two, something new you learned, something you want to do, something you want to change, or just something you want to be sure to remember.

Wisdom to Action
Challenge

In what ways can you cultivate a more reverential fear of the Lord in your daily life? How will this impact your decisions and actions?

Lesson 7
Benefits of Obedience

GENERAL

The question for some is, "Why should I want to be obedient? What do I have to gain? Is it really worth it?" Obviously disobedience is not going to be pleasing to God. You might want to ask, "What must be inherently true if I live in obedience to God's or Christ's commands? What are the real benefits for being obedient? What is the result?"

Let's examine what the Bible says about these questions.

Q1. What do the following verses say about our <u>obedience and faith</u>?

Romans 1:5 We have received grace and apostleship through Him to bring about the obedience of faith among all the nations, on behalf of His name. (HCSB)

Hebrews 5:9 After He was perfected, He became the source of eternal salvation to all who obey Him. (HCSB)

Q2. What do the following verses say about our <u>relationship with Christ</u>?

John 14:15, 21, 23 *"If you love Me, you will keep My commandments. . . . 21 The one who has My commands and keeps them is the one who loves Me. And the one who loves Me will be loved by My Father. I also will love him and will reveal Myself to him." . . . 23 Jesus answered, "If anyone loves Me, he will keep My word. My Father will love him, and We will come to him and make Our home with him."* (HCSB)

2 John 6 *And this is love: that we walk according to His commands. This is the command as you have heard it from the beginning: you must walk in love.* (HCSB)

Q3. What does John 13:34 say about our <u>relationships with one another</u>?

John 13:34 *I give you a new commandment: love one another. Just as I have loved you, you must also love one another.* (HCSB)

Q4. What does 1 John 2 say about our <u>knowing Jesus</u>?

1 John 2:3-4, *This is how we are sure that we have come to know Him: by keeping His commands. 4 The one who says, "I have come to know Him," without keeping His commands, is a liar, and the truth is not in him.*

Q5. What do the following verses say about our <u>relationship with Jesus</u>?

John 8:31 *So Jesus said to the Jews who had believed Him, "If you continue in My word, you really are My disciples."* (HCSB)

1 John 1:4-6 *We are writing these things so that our joy may be complete. 5 Now this is the message we have* *heard from Him and declare to you: God is light, and there is absolutely no darkness in Him. 6 If we say, "We have fellowship with Him," and walk in darkness, we are lying and are not practicing the truth.* (HCSB)

Q6. What is the result of obedience described in the following verses?
John 15:10 *If you keep My commands you will remain [abides] in My love, just as I have kept My Father's commands and remain in His love.* (HCSB)
1 John 3:24 *The one who keeps His commands remains [abides] in Him, and He in him. And the way we know that He remains in us is from the Spirit He has given us.* (HCSB)

Q7. What is the result of obedience described in John 15:14? Is it important?
John 15:14 *You are My friends if you do what I command you.* (HCSB)

Q8. What is the benefit of obedience described in 1 John 3?
1 John 3:22-23 . . . *and receive from him anything we ask,*
because we <u>obey his commands</u> and do what pleases him.
23 And this is his command: to believe in the name of his
Son, Jesus Christ, and to love one another as he
commanded us. (HCSB)

Q9. What is the benefit identified in Luke 11:28?
Luke 11:28 *He said, "Even more, those who hear the word*
of God and keep it are blessed!" (HCSB)

Q10. What are the benefits in the following two verses?
2 Thessalonians 1:8 *taking vengeance with flaming fire on*
those who don't know God and on those who don't obey
the gospel of our Lord Jesus. (HCSB)
Ephesians 5:6 *Let no one deceive you with empty*
arguments, for because of these things God's wrath is
coming on the disobedient. (HCSB)

THE OLD TESTAMENT

It is beneficial to look back at the Old Testament because
there are several benefits associated with obedience
worth noting. While these benefits may vary depending on
the specific context and circumstances, some common
themes emerge throughout the Old Testament.

Q11. In the following passages identify the benefits that result from obedience.

Deuteronomy 28:1-10 *And if you faithfully obey the voice of the Lord your God, being careful to do all his commandments that I command you today, the Lord your God will set you high above all the nations of the earth. 2 And all these blessings shall come upon you and overtake you, if you obey the voice of the Lord your God. 3 Blessed shall you be in the city, and blessed shall you be in the field. 4 Blessed shall be the fruit of your womb and the fruit of your ground and the fruit of your cattle, the increase of your herds and the young of your flock. 5 Blessed shall be your basket and your kneading bowl. 6 Blessed shall you be when you come in, and blessed shall you be when you go out. 7 "The Lord will cause your enemies who rise against you to be defeated before you. They shall come out against you one way and flee before you seven ways. 8 The Lord will command the blessing on you in your barns and in all that you undertake. And he will bless you in the land that the Lord your God is giving you. 9 The Lord will establish you as a people holy to himself, as he has sworn to you, if you keep the commandments of the Lord your God and walk in his ways. 10 And all the peoples of the earth shall see that you are called by the name of the Lord, and they shall be afraid of you.* ESV

Genesis 39:2-6 *The Lord was with Joseph, and . . . 3 His master saw that the Lord was with him and that the Lord caused all that he did to succeed in his hands. 4 So Joseph found favor in his sight and attended him, and he made him overseer of his house and put him in charge of all that*

he had. . . . the blessing of the Lord was on all that he had, in house and field. 6 So he left all that he had in Joseph's charge, and because of him he had no concern about anything but the food he ate. ESV

Psalms 119:165 *Great peace have those who love your law; nothing can make them stumble.* ESV

Psalm 91:9-12 *Because you have made the Lord your dwelling place—the Most High, who is my refuge—10 no evil shall be allowed to befall you, no plague come near your tent. 11 For he will command his angels concerning you to guard you in all your ways. 12 On their hands they will bear you up, lest you strike your foot against a stone.* ESV

Joshua 21:45 *Not one word of all the good promises that the Lord had made to the house of Israel had failed; all came to pass.* ESV

Daniel 12:2-3 *And many of those who sleep in the dust of the earth shall awake, some to everlasting life, and some to shame and everlasting contempt. 3 And those who are wise shall shine like the brightness of the sky above; and those who turn many to righteousness, like the stars forever and ever.* ESV

In summary, we identified various benefits, including divine blessings, favor, peace, protection, fulfillment of promises, and the anticipation of eternal rewards. These benefits should be incentives for individuals to faithfully follow God's commands and live according to His will.

THE NEW TESTAMENT

In the New Testament, obedience to God and adherence to the teachings of Jesus also have positive results. These benefits are often spiritual in nature and focus on the believer's relationship with Jesus, as well as their own personal growth.

Q12. What are the benefits for the believer in the following passages?

John 14:23 *Jesus answered him, "If anyone loves me, he will keep my word, and my Father will love him, and we will come to him and make our home with him.* ESV

2 Peter 1:5-8 *For this very reason, make every effort to supplement your faith with virtue, and virtue with knowledge, 6 and knowledge with self-control, and self-control with steadfastness, and steadfastness with godliness, 7 and godliness with brotherly affection, and brotherly affection with love. 8 For if these qualities are yours and are increasing, they keep you from being ineffective or unfruitful in the knowledge of our Lord Jesus Christ.* ESV

John 8:31-32 *So Jesus said to the Jews who had believed in him, "If you abide in my word, you are truly my disciples, 32 and you will know the truth, and the truth will set you free."* ESV

John 15:10-11 *If you keep my commandments, you will abide in my love, just as I have kept my Father's commandments and abide in his love. 11 These things I have spoken to you, that my joy may be in you, and that your joy may be full.* ESV

1 John 3:22 *and whatever we ask we receive from him, because we keep his commandments and do what pleases him.* ESV

Philippians 2:2-4 *complete my joy by being of the same mind, having the same love, being in full accord and of one mind. 3 Do nothing from rivalry or conceit, but in humility count others more significant than yourselves. 4 Let each of you look not only to his own interests, but also to the interests of others.* ESV

Matthew 19:29 *And everyone who has left houses or brothers or sisters or father or mother or children or lands, for my name's sake, will receive a hundredfold and will inherit eternal life.* ESV

DISCUSSION QUESTIONS

1. For you, what is the most important benefit of living in obedience? Why?

2. Do you consider not conforming to God's commandments as simple disobedience or sinning? Why? Why not?

3. Do you think there is a difference between commands that relate to God compared to those related to how we are to treat one another? Explain.

4. What importance do you associate with abiding? How important is abiding for you in order to walk in obedience? Explain.

5. Do you think we should be concerned about the Old Testament commandments? Why? Why not?

6. How would you explain the freedom we have under the new covenant relative to keeping or ignoring the teachings of Jesus?

CONCLUSION

Obedience to God's will and adherence to the teachings of Christ are associated with spiritual benefits such as intimacy with God, assurance of salvation, spiritual growth, freedom from sin, fulfillment and joy, and effective prayer. These benefits should motivate us to obey God's commands and live according to His teachings.

These benefits highlight the comprehensive impact of obedience to divine instruction, encouraging believers faithfully to follow God's commands and live according to His Word.

WHAT I WANT TO REMEMBER

Enter some notes and information that you want to remember about this lesson. It might be a Scripture verse or two, something new you learned, something you want to do, something you want to change, or just something you want to be sure to remember.

Wisdom to Action
Challenge

How can you align your life more closely with God's commandments this week? What changes will you make to live in a way that truly honors Him?

Lesson 8
Standing Firm

Therefore, my dear brothers, stand firm.
Let nothing move you. Always give yourselves
fully to the work of the Lord . . .
1 Corinthians 15:58 NIV

So then, brothers, stand firm and hold to
the traditions that you were taught by us,
either by our spoken word or by our letter.
2 Thessalonians 2:15 ESV

Anyone who wants to capture or recapture the passion of his faith must do one very important thing when participating in all the activities outlined in the previous lessons of this study: *stand firm!*

You can fix your eyes on Jesus, persevere in prayer, be in the Word, live with integrity, trust in Jesus, abide in Him, be generous, and love Him with all your heart. But if you don't hold fast or stand firm in your faith, if your commitment is in constant flux, if you are only partially faithful, it may not produce the desired result.

It is necessary to recognize that while we are engaged in spiritual activities focused on being right with God, we must be standing firm in our faith. We cannot allow the winds of doubt or the influence of bad friends to nudge us off the narrow path. This is an important concept that cannot be ignored while we are engaged in walking in the ways of God.

STANDING FIRM: Philippians 1:27 – 4:1

There is a long passage in Philippians that talks about how to stand firm. The passage begins in 1:27 where Paul says to "*conduct yourselves in a manner worthy of the gospel of Christ.*" Chapters 2 and 3 provide specific instructions on how to do that and then Paul concludes in 4:1 by saying:

> *Therefore, my brothers . . . <u>stand firm</u> thus in the Lord, my beloved!* ESV

The obvious implication here is that in the prior two chapters Paul has told the Philippians how to stand firm. In verse 2:14-15 we are told to live obedient lives, working out our salvation in order that we may become blameless children of God.

In Philippians 3 Paul says he wants us to obtain the righteousness that comes from God (3:9). Paul follows this by saying he has "*not obtained all this,*" but must press on to take hold of the prize. He then repeats himself in 3:13-14, and says, "*I do not consider myself yet to having taken hold of it.*" Remember, this is all in a passage telling us how to stand firm.

Paul then gives us some excellent advice. He says that if we are not sure of the things he is saying, "*God will make it clear.*" (3:15) I surely can't argue with that advice. I personally do not claim to have all the answers and hope (pray) that God will make it clear to me and all who read this book. Because I too, like Paul, want to stand firm and leave a legacy of making a difference.

The following is a summary from Philippians 1:27 – 4:1 of what Paul says we must do to stand firm:

1:28   do not be frightened by those who oppose the Gospel
1:29   expect to suffer in your Christian walk
2:2   live in unity with other believers
2:3   humbly consider others better than ourselves
2:4   look to the interests of others
2:5   have a selfless attitude, humility, and love of others
2:12a   obey God's commands and instructions
2:12b   work out our salvation with fear and trembling
2:14   do everything without complaining or arguing
2:16   hold out [onto] the word of life
3:1   rejoice in the Lord
3:2   watch out for false teachers
3:3   do not put confidence in our sinful flesh (self)
3:10-14 press on toward goal of knowing Christ; don't look back
3:19   do not have our minds on earthly things
3:20   eagerly await our Savior, the Lord Jesus Christ

Q1. Philippians 3:19 says, "*Their end is destruction, their god is their belly, and they glory in their shame, with minds set on earthly things.*" (ESV) What do you think he is referring to when he says "earthly" things?

What would you do to make sure you stood firm in your faith? Consider what radical things you might think of doing to keep your heart from attaching itself to the values of this world or being focused on earthly things.

There are a number of major worldly values and activities that are inconsistent with our faith:

    1) it's ok if everybody is doing it;
    2) gay marriage;
    3) abortion;
    4) using coarse and vulgar language (God's name in vain);
    5) sex in advertising (sex sells);
    6) promotion of immoral behavior in TV, movies, media;

7) all religious roads lead to the same God;

8) universalism (everyone will be saved);

9) there is no absolute truth; truth is relative;

10) man is inherently good;

11) the real crime is getting caught;

12) you must be tolerate of me – I can do anything I want and you are not permitted to disagree or call me out.

Q2. What do you think is missing from the above?

13) _____

14) _____

15) _____

16) _____

17) _____

18) _____

What must we do in order to protect ourselves and guard our hearts and minds in a crazy world where the overwhelming focus is on self? Some possibilities might include:

MEDIA: Restrict media: magazines, books, newspapers, TV, Internet, movies, podcasts, etc.

MUSIC: Listen exclusively to Christian music or uplifting music.

STUFF: Not own expensive things; drive a Chevy, not a Cadillac.

VALUES: Avoid the trap of adopting the world's values about what is important and what has value. For example we do not have to be politically correct, we do not have to tolerate sinful behavior, and we do not have to remain in the presence of those who use coarse and vulgar language.

FOCUS: Live life for an audience of One, not to please the pagan world and its values.

Q3. At this stage of your life which one of the above options would be the most helpful to you personally? Why?

Q4. Is there something else that would work better for <u>you</u>?

BEING STEADFAST

1 Corinthians 15:58 *Therefore, my beloved brothers, <u>be</u> <u>steadfast</u>, immovable, always abounding in the work of the Lord, knowing that in the Lord your labor is not in vain.* ESV

In 1 Corinthians 15 Paul has been talking about the resurrection and the body of resurrected believers. He ends the chapter with the above verse. He uses some very strong all-inclusive language in describing the act of standing firm or being steadfast:

    a. being immovable,
    b. abounding in the work of the Lord, and
    c. knowing your work is not in vain.

Therefore, if you are allowing something other than Jesus to influence you, if you are only sometimes giving yourself to God's work, or if you are not totally committed to your faith, then you may struggle in your faith.

Being steadfast can be driven by the desire to achieve freedom from arduous requirements and performance rules. But in Christ we can escape the bondage of laws and regulations: Galatians 5:1 tells us, "*It is for freedom that Christ has set us free. Stand firm, then, and do not let yourselves be burdened again by a yoke of slavery.*" NIV

HOW TO STAND FIRM: The armor of God

Paul specifically says in a number of Scriptures that it is by faith that we stand firm. How much faith is required?

What if our faith is weak? In Ephesians 6 Paul says it's going to take more than just simple faith to stand firm:

> *Stand firm then, with the belt of truth buckled around your waist, with the breastplate of righteousness in place, 15 and with your feet fitted with the readiness that comes from the gospel of peace. 16 In addition to all this, take up the shield of faith, with which you can extinguish all the flaming arrows of the evil one. 17 Take the helmet of salvation and the sword of the Spirit, which is the word of God. 18 And pray.* (Ephesians 6:14-18 NIV)

Faith is certainly important, but standing firm seems to be more than simply believing. In Ephesians 6 the broad nature of our obedience and commitment seems far clearer. There are seven things that Paul identifies that constitute putting on the armor of God:

> *1 Belt of Truth:* I acknowledge and accept the Word of God as absolute Truth. I spend time in the Word of God each day.

> *2 Breastplate of Righteousness:* I am in Christ! I know I am covered by the righteousness of Christ. I am a sinner saved by His grace. (2 Corinthians 5:21).

> *3 Shoes of Gospel of Peace:* I accept the Great Commission (Matthew 28:19-20) as my responsibility. I have gospel conversations.

> *4 Shield of Faith:* Jesus is my shield and God is my fortress in overcoming the temptations, trials, or sufferings that challenge my faith (James 1:2-5).

5 Helmet of Salvation: I claim the promises of Scriptures to affirm my salvation. In faith I believe that nothing can separate me from the love of God (Romans 8:38-39).

6 Word of the Spirit: The Word of God is sharper than any double edged-sword (Hebrews 4:12). I pray that it will wash me clean so that I can stand against the evils of this world.

7 Praying in the Spirit: I seek to be filled by the Spirit and for power to pray regularly.

Note that the first five pieces of "armor" are defensive in nature and the last two are offensive. If we are going to stand firm it is going to involve serious work on our part – both defensive and offensive in nature. It's a battle! The meaning here is that all of these things are needed in order to stand firm. Walking in God's ways requires that we are both alert to our needs and diligent in applying God's instructions to our life.

Put on the armor of God!

HOW TO STAND FIRM: Other

In addition to the armor of God, Scripture provides additional guidance on how to stand firm in various contexts. Some are similar to the techniques identified as the armor of God. While the specific instructions may vary depending on the situation, there are principles and practices that can be gleaned from the Scriptures that help us further understand how believers can stand firm in their faith:

1. **Abide in God's Word**
   Jesus teaches in John 8:31-32 that those who hold to His teachings will know the truth, and the truth will set them free. Regular study and meditation on God's Word provides strength, wisdom, and discernment in order to stand firm in the face of trials and temptations.

2. **Be Rooted and Established in Faith**
   Colossians 2:6-7 encourages believers to continue to live their lives in Christ, rooted and built up in Him, strengthened in the faith as they were taught, and overflowing with thankfulness. A deep-rooted faith in Christ helps believers stand firm against doubt and uncertainty.

3. **Pray Continually**
   1 Thessalonians 5:17 urges believers to pray continually. Prayer is a powerful weapon and helps believers stay connected to God, seek His guidance, and find strength to stand firm in difficult times.

Q5. Are you praying enough? What do you need to pray for?

1. **Be Encouraged by Fellow Believers**
   Hebrews 10:24-25 encourages believers to spur one another on toward love and good deeds, and not to give up meeting together, but to encourage one another. Fellowship with other believers provides mutual support, encouragement, and accountability to stand firm in the faith.

2. **Trust in God's Promises**
   Psalm 125:1 declares, *"Those who trust in the Lord are like Mount Zion, which cannot be shaken but endures forever."* (NIV) Trusting in God's promises and faithfulness gives believers confidence and

assurance to stand firm, knowing that God is sovereign and faithful to His word.

Q6. What promise do you need to trust in?

1. **Be Strong and Courageous:** 1 Corinthians 16:13 (NIV) says, *"Be on your guard; stand firm in the faith; be courageous; be strong."* Note that this instruction is given in the context of spiritual warfare.

2. **Resist the Devil:** 1 Peter 5:9 *tells us to stand up to Satan: "Resist him, standing firm in the faith, because you know that the family of believers throughout the world is undergoing the same kind of sufferings."* NIV

Q7. What temptations do you need to resist?

By practicing these principles and relying on the strength and grace of God, you can stand firm in your faith, regardless of the challenges or trials you may face.

NOT STANDING FIRM

If we examine the train of thought for the following verses about not standing firm we find that the consequences are rather significant. We might not be considered disciples, we might not gain life, and we could believe in vain – none of which is a desirable outcome for anyone who is committed to Jesus and wants to be a loyal disciple.

Q8. What do the following passages tell us about not standing firm?

John 8:31 *To the Jews who had believed him, Jesus said, "If you hold to my teaching, you are really my disciples."* NIV

Luke 21:19 *By standing firm you will gain life.* NIV

1 Corinthians 15:2 *By this gospel you are saved, if you hold firmly to the word I preached to you. Otherwise, you have believed in vain.* NIV

We can also observe these same types of warnings and results in Revelation 2-3 where Jesus tells several of the churches to hold on and hold fast or there will be dire consequences.

Lastly we should note Colossians 1:22-23 where the result of not standing firm is that we are not reconciled to Christ:

> *22 . . . He has reconciled you by Christ's physical body through death to present you holy in his sight, without blemish and free from accusation –*
> *23 <u>If you continue in your faith</u>, established and firm, <u>not moved from the hope held out in the gospel</u> . . . NIV*

This passage says both that the Elect will ultimately persevere, and that the Elect are those who do persevere. Such perseverance is the proof of the reality of the Elect. Standing firm and being established in the hope of the gospel is a continuing theme in the New Testament.

If you do not continue in the faith, then you are not reconciled! This would be consistent with what Paul said in 1 Corinthians 15:2 above where the condition is to stand firm in the Word.

The tension between grace, works, and obedience seems to heighten as we read these passages to hold on or stand firm, because if we do not stand firm then any belief was in vain.

In Hebrews 10:23-27 we have another serious warning:

> *Let us hold unswervingly to the hope we profess, for he who promised is faithful. . . . 26 If we deliberately keep on sinning after we have received the knowledge of the truth, no sacrifice for sins is left, 27 but only a <u>fearful expectation of judgment and of raging fire</u> that will consume the enemies of God. NIV*

The author of Hebrews expresses the same kind of warning we have seen above from Paul, John, and Luke. If we hold to the hope we are fine, but if we <u>continue</u> to sin, disobey, rebel, and refuse to repent, it seems there are no options left except the fearful wrath of God. Clearly that is what is in view when the Scripture refers to "judgment, wrath, and raging fire." It has to be a reference to hell.

The only question here might be who the author is talking about, but the context certainly appears to indicate he is addressing those who <u>think</u> they are believers.

Alternatively, it may be to those who have committed apostasy (see 10:28-29). It also may be that some of these warnings passages are intended to highlight the difference between the people attending church and the real church.

WHAT DOES JESUS SAY?

> **Matthew 10:22** *All men will hate you because of me, but he who stands firm to the end will be saved*. NIV

> **Matthew 24:13** *. . . but he who stands firm to the end will be saved*. NIV

> **Revelation 3:11** *I am coming soon. Hold on to what you have, so that no one will take your crown*. NIV

Jesus confirms the importance of standing firm. Those who stand firm to the end will obviously be saved. In Matthew 10 Jesus sends his twelve disciples out to the Israelites with the message, "*The kingdom of heaven is near.*" In both the verses in Matthew Jesus indicates the necessity of persevering "to the end."

This does not say that if you don't stand firm you will not be saved, but if I don't stand firm then I demonstrate that my supposed salvation was not genuine. Clearly the warnings are real because standing firm at the end of the day demonstrates salvation.

Given that we have a number of warnings to stand firm – why do we often ignore the message? Maybe that is what

Jesus is referring to in Revelation 2-3 when he says seven times, "*He who has an ear, let him hear what the Spirit says to the churches.*" Those who do not wish to hear the warnings and reproofs of Revelation 2-3 will not listen to calls for standing firm. Those who do not hear may be inherently rejecting the gospel and giving it only lip service.

Do you have an ear? Are you listening?

CONCLUSION

The above discussion is intended to encourage believers to stand firm in their faith, to remain steadfast in the face of challenges, and to hold fast to the teachings and promises of God. Standing firm implies a posture of strength, courage, and confidence in God's faithfulness and provision. It means being steadfast and unwavering in our commitment to God and His Word, regardless of external circumstances or pressures.

If you are anything like me, you may be overwhelmed with this subject. In this lesson the key phrase is "standing firm" and we see an ongoing and continuing tension.

If grace is all we have, if grace is all we need, if God through the Holy Spirit in His grace is causing us to stand firm, then thanks be to God. But somewhere in this kaleidoscope of inter-mingled requirements, conditions, and calls for standing firm, I hear the message to obey the desires of God or risk my heavenly reward!

It is one thing to have God tell us through His Word how He wants us to act as children of God – I would expect God to do that. But it is another to recognize that passage after passage relates our obedience to receiving the promised hope. Clearly God is telling us that there will be no fake believers in heaven.

DISCUSSION QUESTIONS

1. Reflecting on a time when you faced adversity or opposition, how did you respond? Did you stand firm in your faith, or did you waver? What helped you stand firm? What challenges did you encounter?

2. In 1 Corinthians 15:58, Paul encourages believers to "stand firm. Let nothing move you." What do you think it means to stand firm in your faith, and why is it important? How do you think we must apply this command in our daily lives?

3. Paul frequently exhorts believers to stand firm against spiritual opposition and persecution (e.g., Ephesians 6:13). How do you perceive spiritual warfare in your own life and in the world around you? How do you attempt to stand firm against spiritual attacks?

4. In Galatians 5:1, Paul indicates we should stand firm for our freedom in Christ. How does understanding our freedom impact our ability to resist worldly pressures? How can we avoid falling back into patterns of bondage?

5. Discuss the importance of unity in standing firm as a community of believers. How can we support and encourage one another to stand firm in our faith, especially during times of doubt or difficulty?

6. Do you know anyone who had to stand firm in their faith because they were being tested by the worldly values around them? What could we learn from their experience?

WHAT I WANT TO REMEMBER

Enter some notes and information that you want to remember about this lesson. It might be a Scripture verse or two, something new you learned, something you want to do, something you want to change, or just something you want to be sure to remember.

Wisdom to Action
Challenge

What worldly influences are challenging your faith? How will you actively stand firm in your beliefs and focus on eternal values this week?

Lesson 9
Examples of Biblical Obedience

*You are my friends if you
do what I command.*
John 15:14 NIV

INTRODUCTION

Before we finish this study we will look at some of the examples of obedience and disobedience throughout the pages of Scripture. These examples can give us insight into God's purposes and the importance of being obedient. It can also allow us to see the potential result of rebellion and disobedience on our own lives. We are going to examine several people but it is not our intention to do a deep dive into their lives. Rather we will observe what the Bible says about their obedience or disobedience.

FRIENDSHIP

Before we look at specific characters, it is interesting to note what God says about friendship. In Psalms 25:14 David says, "*The friendship of the Lord is for those who fear him, and he makes known to them his covenant.*" (ESV) This verse indicates that those who have a "fear of the Lord" (hold Him in high regard and reverence) can have a special relationship with God, even to the point of understanding His purposes and covenants.

The Bible identifies Abraham and Moses specifically as friends of God. (2 Chronicles 20:7 and Exodus 33:11). We will examine these two further, after our discussion on friends. While the term "friend" isn't explicitly used, David's close relationship with God is evident throughout the Psalms. He is referred to as "a man after God's own heart" in Acts 13:22 (NIV).

Jesus calls His disciple friends. Notice what John reports that Jesus said:

> **John 15:14-15** *You are my friends if you do what I command. I no longer call you servants, because a servant does not know his master's business. Instead, I have called you friends, for everything that I learned from my Father I have made known to you.* NIV

Jesus said that His friends are obedient, and there is the strong implication that one cannot be a friend unless you walk in His ways and obey His commands. "Friendship" with God must carry special importance since only a few biblical characters are specifically identified as being friends of God.

While the Bible explicitly identifies those identified above as friends, there are certainly several others whose lives exemplified a close and intimate relationship with God/Jesus, even if the term "friend" isn't directly used:

1. **Enoch** "walked faithfully with God" and was taken by God, implying a deep relationship. This is highlighted in Genesis 5:24 and Hebrews 11:5.

2. **Noah** "walked with God," indicating a personal relationship marked by faithfulness and obedience (Genesis 6:9).

3. **Samuel** had a unique role as a prophet and judge, and his close communication with God is evidence of a close relationship.

4. **Daniel's** faithfulness and consistent prayer life show a profound relationship with God. The stories of his courage and divine deliverance highlight God's favor and closeness to him.

5. **Mary** the mother of Jesus, while not called a friend, her deep faith and obedience exemplify a very close relationship to her Son.

6. **Paul's** writings highlight his deep connection and commitment to Christ, reflecting an intimate and transformative friendship.

These examples demonstrate that a close relationship with God, characterized by trust and obedience is a common theme throughout the Bible, even if the term "friend" isn't specifically used.

ABRAHAM

One of the most amazing accounts of obedience in the Bible occurs when God asked Abraham to sacrifice his only son (the son of promise):

> **Genesis 22:2** *He said, "Take your son, your only son Isaac, whom you love, and go to the land of Moriah, and offer him there as a burnt offering on one of the mountains of which I shall tell you." ESV*

This was a staggering faith commitment and unbelievable act of obedience! History demonstrates that God does not test everyone as He tested Abraham. But from this story we come to understand that God absolutely desires our worship (the sacrifice) and our obedience. As in the case of friendship above, the obedience of Abraham is linked to fearing God. The resulting blessing is a result of that obedience:

> He said, "Do not lay your hand on the boy or do anything to him, for now I know that you fear God, seeing you have not withheld your son, your only son, from me . . . 18 and in your offspring shall all the nations of the earth be blessed, because you have obeyed my voice."
> (Genesis 22:12, 18 and 26:4-5 ESV]

Abraham is often referred to as the Father of Faith for his unwavering trust and obedience to God. He demonstrated remarkable faith and trust when he obeyed God's call to leave his homeland and journey to a land God had not yet shown him (Genesis 12:1). Despite not knowing where he was going, Abraham immediately obeyed God's command and thus became the patriarch of Israel. His willingness to sacrifice his son Isaac, in obedience to God's command, further demonstrated his faith and obedience.

We should not leave the example of Abraham without noting 2 Chronicles 20:7 where Abraham's relationship is again related to friendship: "*O our God, did you not drive out the inhabitants of this land before your people Israel and give it forever to the descendants of Abraham your friend?*" NIV

Q1. In your opinion which is the most critical issue for Abraham: fearing God or obedience?

DAVID

David is described as a man after God's own heart (1 Samuel 12:14). We learn the reason for that statement in Acts 13:22, which tells us why God felt this way:

> *After removing Saul, he made David their king. He testified concerning him: 'I have found David son of Jesse a man after my own heart; he will do everything I want him to do.'* NIV

God described David as a "man after my own heart" because David would obey – he would do what God asked him to do. We certainly need to come to God in fear and trembling (reverent fear), we absolutely need to revere Him, we should be in awe of Him, humble ourselves before Him, and understand that He is the ultimate source of knowledge and wisdom. But Scripture continually repeats that the key to a right relationship with God is obedience:

> *"Blessed is the man who fears the LORD, who finds great delight in his commands."* (Psalm 112:1 NIV)

David was identified as a man who had God's favor because he was obedient. Obedience pleases the heart of God! As Christ-followers we live lives of obedience either because we (1) are grateful for God's grace, or (2) recognize that our God is an awesome God whom we should serve in "fear and trembling." If we choose to rebel against God's commandments, we risk punishment:

> *And Samuel said to Saul, "You have done foolishly. You have not kept the command of the Lord your God, with which he commanded you. For then the Lord would have established your kingdom over Israel forever. 14 But now your kingdom shall not continue. The Lord has sought out a man after his*

own heart, and the Lord has commanded him to
be prince over his people, because you have not
kept what the Lord commanded you."
(1 Samuel 13:13-14 ESV)

MOSES

Moses also had a special relationship with God: *The LORD would speak to Moses face to face, as a man speaks with his friend* . . . (Exodus 33:11 NIV). Psalm 103:7 reminds the reader that God made His ways known to Moses when they spoke face to face.

Moses is known for his obedience to God's call to deliver the Israelites from slavery in Egypt. Despite his initial reluctance and feelings of inadequacy, Moses obeyed God's command to confront Pharaoh and demand the release of the Israelites. He faithfully led Israel throughout the wilderness for forty years, despite facing numerous challenges, setbacks, and the grumbling of the people, who never seemed to be satisfied. Moses' obedience to God's commands ultimately led to the liberation of the Israelites and the establishment of the Mosaic covenant that they received through Moses at Mount Sinai.

DANIEL and Shadrach, Meshach, and Abednego

Daniel is known for his unwavering faithfulness to God and his commitment to Him even in the face of great adversity. After being taken captive and shipped off to Babylon he remained steadfast in his faith and commitment to God. Despite facing persecution and pressure to compromise his beliefs, Daniel remained obedient and refused to bow down to idols or abandon his prayer habits. God rewarded Daniel's faithfulness by delivering him from the den of lions and elevating him to a position of influence in the Babylonian and Persian empires.

Shadrach, Meshach, and Abednego were three young men, who along with Daniel, were taken captive to Babylon. The three are known for their refusal to bow down and worship the golden image set up by King Nebuchadnezzar. Despite the threat of being thrown into a fiery furnace, Shadrach, Meshach, and Abednego remained steadfast in their faith, declaring their trust in God's ability to deliver them. Even when faced with certain death, they stood firm in their obedience to God, and God miraculously rescued them from the flames.

The three may be best known for their response to King Nebuchadnezzar when the King demanded they worship the man-made image:

> **Daniel 3:16-18** *Shadrach, Meshach, and Abednego answered and said to the king, "O Nebuchadnezzar, we have no need to answer you in this matter. 17 If this be so, our God whom we serve is able to deliver us from the burning fiery furnace, and he will deliver us out of your hand, O king. 18 But if not, be it known to you, O king, that we will not serve your gods or worship the golden image that you have set up." ESV*

Q2. What do you think is required in a relationship with God that would allow a follower to give such a response in the face of death?

ESTHER

Esther was a Jewish orphan, raised by her cousin Mordecai, who became queen of Persia during a time of great peril for her people. Haman, the king's advisor, plotted to exterminate the Jewish population and Mordecai urged Esther to intercede on behalf of her people. She risked her own life in the process, but despite the danger, Esther courageously obeyed Mordecai's instructions, approached the king uninvited, and appealed for mercy for her people.

Through Esther's obedience and bravery, God intervened to save the Jewish people from extinction. His promise of a future for Israel remained undeterred. God used a Jewish orphan who was faithful to protect the Jewish nation and accomplish His plans.

PAUL

Paul, formerly a persecutor of Christians under the name of Saul, encountered the risen Jesus on the road to Damascus. After his conversion, Paul became a devoted follower of Christ and a fearless advocate for the gospel. Despite facing intense persecution and imprisonment, Paul remained steadfast in his obedience to God's call to preach the gospel to the Gentiles. His obedience to God's directions and instructions caused him to endure hardships, beatings, and imprisonment, but he never wavered in his commitment to spreading the message of salvation, particularly to the Gentiles.

Q3. Can you identify one or more situations when Paul was obedient to the Holy Spirit or God's direction and he found himself in great danger?

NOAH

Noah is known for his obedience to God's command to build an ark and prepare for a flood, even though it seemed irrational to others. Despite facing ridicule and mockery from his neighbors, Noah faithfully followed God's instructions and saved his family and pairs of animals from The Flood that destroyed the earth. His obedience to God's command preserved the human race and set an example of faithfulness for us today.

Hebrews 11:7 describes this story saying that Noah, in holy fear, built an ark to save his family. It should be remembered that the ark took nearly 100 years to build. That has to be some kind of record for being obedient!

RUTH

Ruth, a Moabite woman, demonstrated remarkable loyalty and obedience to God by choosing to accompany her mother-in-law Naomi back to Israel after the death of her husband. Despite the cultural and social challenges she faced as a foreigner in Israel, Ruth remained devoted to Naomi and embraced the God of Israel as her own. Through her obedience and faithfulness, Ruth became an ancestor of King David and ultimately of Jesus Christ.

JOB

Job is known for his unwavering perseverance, even in the midst of intense suffering and adversity. Despite losing his wealth, health, and family, Job refused to curse God or turn away from Him. Instead, he remained steadfast in his faith, declaring, "*Though he slay me, yet will I hope in him*" (Job 13:15, NIV). Through his obedience and trust in God, Job ultimately experienced restoration and blessing.

Q4. You may have heard the expression, "the patience of Job." Why is this expression incorrect?

OBSCURE CHARACTERS

While many of the more prominent characters in the Bible are well-known for their obedience or for standing firm in their faith, there are also lesser-known individuals whose stories offer valuable lessons and inspiration.

These lesser-known individuals may not receive as much attention as some of the more prominent figures in the Bible, but their stories of obedience, faithfulness, and courage offer valuable insights and inspiration. They demonstrate that obedience to God and standing firm in your faith can be demonstrated in various roles and circumstances, and that even seemingly obscure individuals can play a significant role in God's plans. The OBSCURE Bible Study Series, described at the end of this book, contains the stories of 68 obscure biblical characters that significantly impacted history.

Phinehas

Phinehas was a priest during the time of Moses and Joshua. He is known for his zealous obedience to God and his actions to stop a rebellion against God's commands. When some Israelite men were led astray by Moabite women and began engaging in idolatry and immorality, Phinehas took decisive action by spearheading an act of judgment that stopped a plague of judgment and restored God's favor (Numbers 25:1-13).

Phinehas' zealous obedience to God's commands and his willingness to take a stand for righteousness are amazing examples of being faithful and obedient.

Obadiah

Obadiah was a servant of King Ahab of Israel. He secretly harbored reverence for God and helped to protect and provide for the prophets during a time of persecution (1 Kings 18:3-4). Despite the risks involved, Obadiah remained faithful to God and demonstrated compassion and courage in protecting God's chosen prophets. His quiet obedience and commitment to righteousness serve as a reminder that even in times of darkness and opposition, there are those who remain faithful and obedient to God's commands.

Huldah the Prophetess

Huldah was a prophetess who lived during the reign of King Josiah of Judah. When Josiah sought guidance from God after the Book of the Law was rediscovered in the temple, he sent a delegation to consult with Huldah.

Despite living in a predominantly male-dominated society, Huldah fearlessly delivered a message from God, affirming Josiah's obedience to God's commands and foretelling judgment upon Judah for their disobedience (2 Kings 22:14-20, 2 Chronicles 34:22-28). Huldah's obedience indicates that God can use individuals of any background or status to fulfill His purposes and speak His truth.

Onesiphorus:

Onesiphorus is mentioned briefly in the New Testament as a faithful supporter and encourager of the apostle Paul. In 2 Timothy 1:16-18, Paul expresses gratitude for Onesiphorus' loyal friendship and describes how he sought out Paul in Rome and refreshed him while he was in prison. Despite the risk and inconvenience involved, Onesiphorus demonstrated selfless obedience to God by ministering to Paul in his time of need. Onesiphorus' demonstrated support to fellow believers, even in difficult circumstances.

Hymenaeus

There are also examples of disobedience. Paul identified several people who were creating problems in the faith community. One of them was Hymenaeus who was mentioned in both letters to Timothy:

1 Timothy 1:19-20 . . . *By rejecting this, some have made shipwreck of their faith, 20 among whom are* _Hymenaeus_ *and Alexander, whom I have handed over to Satan that they may learn not to blaspheme.* ESV

2 Timothy 2:14-17 *Remind them . . . not to quarrel about words, which does no good, . . . present yourself to God . . . rightly handling the word of truth. 16 But avoid irreverent babble, for it will lead people into more and more ungodliness, 17 and their talk will spread like gangrene. Among them are* _Hymenaeus_ *and Philetus,* ESV

Paul was very concerned about doctrine and he encouraged Timothy to stand firm:

> **2 Timothy 4:2** *preach the word; be ready in season and out of season; reprove, rebuke, and exhort, with complete patience and teaching.* ESV

Paul warned Timothy that some followers had rejected the truth, resulting in their faith being "shipwrecked." Paul said he handed Hymenaeus over to Satan in order to be taught not to blaspheme. Blasphemy in the Old Testament was a crime punishable by death (Lev 24:15-16). It meant that God was being cursed or slandered in some way. The offense exhibited an obvious contempt for God and His precepts.

Paul goes on to say that Hymenaeus had wandered away or deviated from the truth. Apparently Hymenaeus claimed that the resurrection had already taken place, probably implying that there is no bodily resurrection, only a spiritual one. The result was that he and his cohorts caused others to believe their heresy and destroy the faith of those being led astray.

Wandering away from the faith can often begin with baby steps. We are not really intending to abandon our faith but the faith connection is broken and non-participation leads to a cooling off of desire for righteousness to the point you find yourself a long way off and very difficult to re-connect. This may not have been the original intent but it occurs slowly over time and one day you wake up and the distance is like looking out over a vast ocean, not a little meandering brook.

Q5. Do you know or have you heard of anyone like Hymenaeus? How do you react to these kind of people? How do you think they should they be treated?

Q6. What does it mean when Paul says in 1 Timothy 1:20 that he handed Hymenaeus over to Satan?

Q7. What do you think it means when Paul says in 2 Timothy 2:18 that Hymenaeus had "swerved from the truth"?

DISCUSSION QUESTIONS

1. How do the experiences of these biblical characters illustrate the various ways in which individuals can demonstrate obedience and faithfulness to God? Which character or story is most meaningful to you? Why?

2. What common traits or qualities do you observe among the characters who stood firm and followed God's commands? How do these traits contribute to their ability to remain faithful in challenging circumstances?

3. In what ways do the stories of these characters inspire or challenge your own faith journey? Are there aspects of their experiences that resonate with your own life? Explain.

4. Reflecting on these stories, what lessons or principles can we glean for navigating difficult situations or remaining steadfast in our commitment to God?

5. Many of these characters would have faced moments of doubt, fear, or temptation. What can we learn from their examples in dealing with our own fears?

6. Reflect on the impact of obedience and faithfulness. In which examples did the actions of these characters influence future generations and shape the course of biblical history?

7. How do the stories of these characters challenge or support your understanding of obedience and faithfulness in contemporary society?

CONCLUSION

These Biblical characters demonstrated obedience and the ability to stand firm in their faith despite adversity. God's power comes from trusting in Him. Their stories can inspire believers to remain faithful to God's commands, even in the face of challenges and trials.

These examples highlight the diverse ways in which individuals throughout the Bible demonstrated obedience and stood firm in their faith, serving as inspiring examples for us today.

WHAT I WANT TO REMEMBER

Enter some notes and information that you want to remember about this lesson. It might be a Scripture verse or two, something new you learned, something you want to do, something you want to change, or just something you want to be sure to remember.

Wisdom to Action
Challenge

How can you deepen your trust in God's character and promises? What act of obedience will you undertake to strengthen your friendship with God?

Lesson 10
Summary

PART A – 15 KEY COMMANDMENTS

If we are to "stand firm" we need an understanding of what we must resist and what we should embrace. The Bible includes references to many commands, instructions, requirements, and warnings for the Jesus follower.

We know that keeping Jesus' commands is important because in John 14:15 He said, "*If you love me, keep my commands.*" Obedience to God's commandments is an expression of our love for Him. While we are saved by grace through faith, obedience is the required and natural response to our love, trust, and gratitude towards God.

KEY COMMANDS

We have gathered a list of commands or requirements in the Bible. This is not meant to be a comprehensive list but it covers many of the most important commands. We have made no attempt to put these in any order but we would guess the first six have to be pretty near the top of anyone's priority list.

1. **Love God**: Jesus emphasized the greatest commandment in Matthew 22:37-38, saying it was to love the Lord with all your heart, soul, and mind. Jesus said this is the first and greatest commandment. Loving God involves wholehearted devotion, worship, and surrender to Him.

2. **Love Others**: Jesus also said in Matthew 22:39 that the second greatest commandment was to love your neighbor as yourself. Loving others involves showing kindness, compassion, and forgiveness towards others. We are to

treat others as we would like to be treated. There are no exceptions for enemies or people we don't like.

3. **Follow Jesus**: Jesus called people to follow Him as His disciples. In Matthew 16:24, He said that anyone who wanted to be a disciple should deny themselves, take up their cross, and follow Him. Following Jesus means surrendering our lives to Him, obeying His teachings, and seeking to follow His ways.

4. **Salvation:** There are a number of important commands related to salvation:

- **Confess Jesus as Lord:** Romans 10:9 *"If you declare with your mouth, 'Jesus is Lord,' and believe in your heart that God raised him from the dead, you will be saved."* NIV
- **Be Born Again:** John 3:3 *"Jesus replied, 'Very truly I tell you, no one can see the kingdom of God unless they are born again.'"* NIV
- **Receive the Holy Spirit:** Acts 2:38 *"Peter replied, 'Repent and be baptized, every one of you, in the name of Jesus Christ for the forgiveness of your sins. And you will receive the gift of the Holy Spirit.'"* NIV
- **Stand Firm:** Matthew 24:13 *"but the one who stands firm to the end will be saved."* NIV
- **Abide in Christ:** John 15:4 *"Remain in me, as I also remain in you. No branch can bear fruit by itself; it must remain in the vine. Neither can you bear fruit unless you remain in me."* NIV
- **Work Out Your Salvation:** Philippians 2:12 *"Therefore, my dear friends, as you have always obeyed—not only in my presence, but now much more in my absence— continue to work out your salvation with fear and trembling."* NIV

5. **Faith and Belief**: Hebrews 11:6 says that without faith it is impossible to please God. Anyone who has faith must believe that He exists. Faith is an essential requirement for

salvation, trusting in God's promises, and believing in Jesus as Savior and Lord.

6. **Our Priority is seeking Him:** Matthew 6:33 tells us the first thing to do is seek His kingdom and His righteousness. If we do that, then our needs will be supplied.

7. **Repentance:** Throughout the Bible, repentance is emphasized as a requirement for followers of God. Acts 3:19 states that we must repent and turn toward God. Repentance involves acknowledging our sins, turning away from them, and seeking forgiveness and transformation through His grace.

8. **Serve Others:** Mark 10:45 says that Jesus came to serve, not to be served. We are to do likewise. Jesus washed the disciples' feet to demonstrate and teach them this lesson.

9. **Be Active Doers of the Word:** James 1:22 tells us to do what the Word says. We should not only read it, but do it.

10. **Prayer**: In 1 Thessalonians 5:17, Paul instructs believers to "pray continually." Prayer is a means of communication with God, seeking His guidance, expressing our needs and desires, and growing in our relationship with Him.

11. **Forgive:** Jesus says in Matthew 6:14-15 that if we do not forgive other people when they sin against us, then God will not forgive us. Forgiveness is a commandment that emphasizes the importance of extending grace and mercy to others, just as God has forgiven us.

12. **Share the Gospel/Teach Disciples:** Jesus gave the Great Commission to His disciples in Matthew 28:19-20, indicating they were to go and make disciples, baptizing in the name of the Father, Son, and Holy Spirit. We are to teach disciples to obey everything Jesus commanded. That is a big responsibility!

13. **Be Holy:** 1 Peter 1:16 indicates we are to be holy, just as the godhead is holy.

14. **Act Justly, Love Mercy, Walk Humbly**: Micah 6:8 states, "*He has told you, O man, what is good; and what does the Lord require of you but to do justice, and to love kindness, and to walk humbly with your God?*" (ESV) This command highlights the importance of pursuing justice, standing up for the oppressed, caring for the poor, disadvantaged, and needy, while living surrendered to God. A broad interpretation of these three requirements does not leave us much else to do!

15. **Ten Commandments:** All but the Sabbath requirement apply to the New Testament church, including:

- Honor Parents: Exodus 20:12,
- Do Not Steal: Exodus 20:15
- Do Not Bear False Witness: Exodus 20:16
- Do Not Covet: Exodus 20:17

These 15 commands and instructions highlight the ethical and moral principles that guide the lives of believers. By following these commands, believers strive to live in accordance with God's will and demonstrate love and righteousness in their relationships and actions to the watching world.

Wisdom to Action
Challenge

Which of these principles (love, obedience, faith, repentance, service) needs more attention in your life? How will you practically apply it this week?

PART B – IMPLEMENTATION

MAKING PROGRESS

How are you doing? Are you making progress? There are several benchmarks you can keep in mind in order to make obedience a high priority in our life:

1. Obedience is the end game

Obeying God's laws and precepts must be an overriding consideration for most every decision we make. We must continually think about whether our actions fit with God and His commandments.

2. Obedience is immediate

When the Spirit of God speaks, we need to respond immediately. Partial or delayed obedience is not obedience.

3. Obedience is God's will

An obedient Jesus follower desires to learn more about God, His desires, His works and His plans. Certainly we will never know all there is to know about God and His will, but spiritual knowledge helps shape our life and direct our walk. It keeps us on the right path. Seeking the knowledge of God's ways (His will) means we do not ask God to bless our plans, but we ask God what His plans are for us so we can be a blessing.

4. Obedience must be a high priority

The world and others do not take priority over the plans of God. The obedient person has no concern whether others may reject or ridicule him. The only real test is, "What does God say?" The Jesus follower seeks out the wisdom of other people, but he does not act based on human consensus. He commits to what God requires, even against the advice of others.

5. Obedience has consequences

An obedient person is willing to suffer the "slings and arrows of outrageous fortune" if necessary. No Christian is eager to suffer, but we can be joyful in the midst of it. Remember what Jesus taught in the Beatitudes: *"Blessed are those who are persecuted because of righteousness, for theirs is the kingdom of heaven."* (Matthew 5:10 NIV)

Summary

Everything we do that builds spiritual discipline or spiritual growth is in some way founded on obedience. We pray, for example, because God commands it. We read and study the Bible because God desires that we know and obey His commands. We take time alone because He says, *"Be still, and know that I am God . . ."* (Psalm 46:10) God knows what we need and what will produce His purposes in our life. We simply must be intentional.

BEING INTENTIONAL

We must recognize the desire of the Lord is that we walk in His ways. Generally when we are obedient He empowers us with the ability to perform according to His commandments.

Key facts about biblical obedience:

1. Expected From the Beginning: Obedience was expected from the beginning. Deuteronomy 10:12-13 said *"And now, Israel, what does the Lord your God require of you, but to fear the Lord your God, to walk in all his ways, to love him, to serve the Lord your God with all your heart and with all your soul, 13 and to keep the commandments and statutes of the Lord, which I am commanding you today for your good?"* ESV

2. <u>Chosen For Obedience</u>: 1 Peter 1:2 says that we are chosen by God for obedience to Jesus Christ.

3. <u>The Requirement</u>: Jesus said in Matthew 19:17 that if we wanted to enter life we were to obey the commandments, which was the requirement for being right with God in the Old Testament.

4. <u>Teach the Disciples to Obey</u>: The Great Commission in Matthew 28:20 told us that we are not only supposed to go and baptize but to teach disciples to obey everything Jesus had commanded.

5. <u>God's Wrath</u>: Ephesians warned us that God's wrath will come on those who are disobedient.

SUMMARY: Even in this limited review, it is easy to conclude that obedience is a cornerstone of being a true Christ follower. Our *inability* to live in perfect obedience in this life clearly *demonstrates God's grace*. God wants our perfect obedience but in His wisdom He understands our inability to achieve that "perfect" state on our own, therefore, He provides us grace through Christ and the work of the Holy Spirit to help us be the people He wants us to be.

HOW TO OBEY

These are two practical steps for the reader who wants to know what to do and how to be intentional about being obedient.

1. Desire to change in your life
Decide you want more and desire to be really committed to your faith, then commit to doing something about it. But it is more than recognizing the need. We must really be committed. Saying we are committed to something and

being absolutely committed in our hearts to act are often two different things! You have to want it!

2. Pray fervently for life-change!
We should be praying for things that impact eternity. Praying fervently means we are zealous to walk in His ways and have a high desire to obey. We pray passionately for a life that is pleasing to God. We pray for humility, holiness, righteousness, faithfulness, compassion, and to be conformed to the likeness of Christ. We are in earnest, and persistent prayer. We do not give up until we have God's attention!

CONCLUSION

Obedience is a central theme throughout the entire Bible, including both Testaments. It includes the act of submitting to God's authority, following His commands, and aligning one's words and actions with His will. It is portrayed as essential for creating a right relationship with Him in order to receive His blessings and fulfill His purposes.

In the Old Testament, obedience is often linked with the concept of covenant—a sacred agreement between God and His people. Living in obedience entailed keeping the covenant promises the people (nation) made with God. The Israelites were called to obey God's laws and commandments in the Sinai Covenant given to the people through Moses. Keeping the Law was the key to experiencing His blessings and prosperity in the Promised Land.

The wisdom literature of the Old Testament, including the books of Psalms, Proverbs, and Ecclesiastes, also highlighted the value of obedience in living a wise and fulfilling life. Proverbs provides practical advice for living according to the virtues of God. The wisdom in Proverbs is portrayed as the path to success, prosperity, and righteousness. Ecclesiastes ultimately concludes that obedience to God's commands is the whole duty of man (the essence of man's existence) which will produce a meaningful and purposeful life.

In the New Testament, obedience takes on new dimensions in light of the redemptive work of Christ. Followers are called to obey the teachings of Jesus and follow His example, demonstrating their love for Him through their obedience. Jesus Himself displayed perfect obedience to the will of the Father, even unto death on the cross. He demonstrated the ultimate model for believers to emulate.

The Apostle Paul emphasized the importance of obedience in the Christian life, describing it within the context of grace and salvation. While salvation is received by grace through faith in Christ, obedience is presented as evidence of genuine faith and a right relationship with God. We are called to "walk in obedience" (2 John 1:6), living out their faith in practical obedience to God's commands.

The New Testament also warns against the consequences of disobedience and falling away from the faith. Hebrews, for example, cautions believers against drifting away from the truth and encourages them to persevere in faith and obedience. While believers are assured of God's forgiveness and grace, the Bible reiterates the importance of continuing in obedience to experience the fullness of God's blessings and eternal life.

Obedience is rooted in love for God and demonstrated through faithful adherence to His commands. It is the path to intimacy with God, spiritual growth, and fulfillment of His purposes for our lives. As believers strive to walk in obedience, they experience the transformative power of

God's grace, enabling them to live in accordance with His will and bring glory to His name.

CAUTION: Relationship Over Obedience

We must not forget that the primary call on our life is not to performance or activity – it's first and foremost to follow Him, to abide in Him, and to know Him. It's all about intimacy and relationship because He wants us to be in fellowship with Him. The purpose of the relationship is to know God, and thus we must spend time with Him developing that relationship.

An all-consuming determination to obey can become overwhelming, exhausting, and burdensome. We simply cannot do enough or be consistent enough in our earthly life to please God (complete obedience). There is no freedom, peace, or rest in trying to live the Christian life through absolute obedience, because too much guilt is produced in failing to live up to God's standard or one's own expectations. Our primary goal must be the relationship, not the activity that is produced from that relationship. Through relationship we are set free from the bondage of performance.

John 14:15 says that *"If you love me, you will keep my commands."* Unfortunately most of us put the emphasis on the second half of that statement – that's easy to do. But obedience will flow out of the love. Thus, in our daily walk we typically don't have an obedience problem – we have a *love* problem. I love me more than I love God, and my obedience to Christ suffers in direct proportion to the weakness of my love for Him.

In the Old Testament it was appropriate to ask what the Lord required of me (Malachi 6:8) because salvation was based on obedience to the law (which was intended to ultimately point the people forward to the cross and Jesus). But with the coming of Christ, asking what is required of me is no longer the applicable question. Salvation is by faith – it is a gift of God's grace. Religious activity (performance) is not a requirement for salvation. Thus, obedience, although extremely important, is not required to gain or maintain salvation: we are saved by the blood of the Lamb.

DISCUSSION QUESTIONS

1. Do you agree with the conclusion above? If not, why not?

2. What are you struggling with in regard to obedience? How could your study group help you?

3. In reviewing the 15 important commands we listed at the beginning of this lesson, what did we miss? Can you identify a command that you think should be included on that list? Explain why.

4. We listed two major steps under "HOW TO OBEY." What would you add to desire and prayer?

5. How do you interpret the command to "love God with all your heart, soul, and mind" (Matthew 22:37)? What practical steps could we take to express this kind of love in our daily lives?

6. In what practical ways could we demonstrate love for our one another, especially those who may be difficult to love? How does the command to love others challenge our natural inclinations?

7. How do you personally reconcile or harmonize the concepts of God's grace and man's obedience in your faith journey? Why do you think obedience is emphasized as a response to love in John 14:15?

8. Reflecting on Mark 10:45, how can we embody a servant attitude in our families or communities? What are some practical ways to serve others that align with Jesus' examples in these two groups?

9. What do you think it means to be holy as God is holy (1 Peter 1:16)? How can we pursue holiness in a world that often promotes contrary values?

WHAT I WANT TO REMEMBER

Enter some notes and information that you want to remember about this lesson. It might be a Scripture verse or two, something new you learned, something you want to do, something you want to change, or just something you want to be sure to remember.

Wisdom to Action
Challenge

How can you cultivate a greater sense of reverential awe and respect for God in your daily life? What impact will this have on your purpose and actions?

Appendix A
Faith, Works, and Security

We found an excellent overview of faith, good works, and eternal security on the "gotquestions.org" website. We believe that this may help you understand the relationship between these concepts and the current theological thinking. The following is copied directly:

There are four basic approaches to the issues surrounding faith, works, and security. The first approach is to say that you must have faith and continued obedience to be saved. You will not know for sure that you're saved until you die and your life is finally evaluated by God. Then you will be saved or lost based on your performance in life. This is the basic teaching of the Roman Catholic Church as well as the thought of many Protestants. However, this approach does not adequately explain the teaching of Scripture that we are saved by grace through faith and that salvation is something that takes place here and now—not just in the afterlife.

The second approach to the relationship of faith, works, and security says that you are saved by faith to the exclusion of works. In this line of thinking, if you profess faith in Christ and subsequently repudiate your faith or embrace gross sin, you are still saved, because you are saved no matter what you do. This approach, sometimes called "easy believism," does not take seriously the warnings in Scripture that emphasize personal holiness and enduring faith.

The third approach to faith, works, and security states that you are saved by faith, but you must somehow maintain your salvation through a combination of faith and works—or at least you must avoid flagrant, unrepentant sin. In other words, you may be saved, justified, born again, adopted into God's family, and indwelt with the Holy Spirit yet still fall away and ultimately be lost. While this approach does take seriously Scripture's warnings against sin, it still does not properly account for the many passages that speak of assurance of salvation, not to mention that we are saved apart from our works.

The final approach to faith, works, and security affirms that you are saved by faith based on the merit of Jesus Christ who died for you. In a great exchange, your sin was placed on Christ, and His righteousness was placed on you. The result of being born again and indwelt with God's Spirit is that He begins to change you from the inside out. Your inner change becomes outwardly visible by continued faith and increasing obedience. If you profess faith in Christ but offer no evidence of a changed life, we have good reason to suspect that your initial profession may not have been genuine (Matthew 7:21).

The first approach fails because it adds works to faith as the means of salvation and denies security. The second approach fails because it ignores the need for a changed life (see Ephesians 1:4). The third approach fails because it places on us the duty of maintaining salvation instead of on Christ where it belongs (see Galatians 1:1–3). The fourth and final approach is biblical. We are saved by faith, not by our own good works (Ephesians 2:8–9), yet we are saved to do good works (Ephesians 2:10).

The belief here is that the Elect persevere because God keeps the believer connected and enables him to persevere. (Philippians 1:6).

Source: https://www.gotquestions.org/faith-works-security.html <NoV. 2024>

Wisdom to Action
Challenge

What good works, empowered by the Holy Spirit, can you engage in this week as evidence of your transformed life in Christ?

Transformation Road Map

Primary Takeaways

1: Obedience to God's Word is fundamental to a Christian's faith walk, enabling spiritual growth, empowering ministry, and fostering intimacy with God. This is in contrast to a culture that often prioritizes tolerance and relative truth over absolute obedience.

2: God does require obedience from His followers! This obedience stems from a deep love and reverence for God, encompassing all aspects of a believer's life and serving as the foundation for a meaningful relationship with the Divine.

3: Obedience to God, although an essential aspect of genuine faith, is *not* as a means to earn salvation. It is only evidence of a transformed life and a loving relationship with God.

4: God may test believers to reveal their strengths and weaknesses or their persistent disobedience and rebellion against His commands. Disobedience can lead to punishment or disciplinary measures intended for correction, restoration, and spiritual growth.

5: A Christian's faith walk necessitates a growing love relationship with Jesus, demonstrated through obedience to His commands indicating a true commitment to following Him.

6: Our faith walk should be characterized by a reverential fear of the Lord, which involves awe, respect, and obedience to Christ's commandments, recognizing His authority and sovereignty.

7: Obedience to God must be the foundation of Christian living. Such obedience leads to a life of purpose, meaning, and eternal joy.

8: A Christian's faith walk requires standing firm in our beliefs, resisting doubt and worldly influences. We must actively work out our salvation through obedience, humility, and a focus on eternal values.

9: Our obedience should come from love and confidence in God's character and His promises. Obedience is essential for a relationship with God and for fulfilling our purpose in life.

10: Christian faith and good works, empowered by the Holy Spirit, serve as evidence of a genuine transformed life and a secure relationship with God.

What are you being called to do next?

Leader Guide

This Guide is designed to give a leader answers and additional information to effectively lead a discussion of each lesson in this book.

Tips For Leading

We recommend that you begin a group discussion by reading an appropriate Scripture. It may be one that you will cover in the material or another related passage you have chosen. This will do several things:

- Allow time for everyone to get settled.
- Remind everyone of the subject and bring their minds to a common focus.
- Provide a transition from the previous activity.

Additional ice-breakers are usually not necessary, but if your group is new or members don't know each other well, you could have someone give their testimony/story at the beginning of each week. If you sense that the group needs additional focus before you begin with the discussion, conduct a short discussion about the themes of the lesson or ask about the meaning of a particular term associated with the lesson.

Goals

The discussion should center around the questions in the lesson. But remember that each person in your group has different goals and is at a different place in his or her Christian walk. Jesus may be an old friend to some but a new acquaintance to others. The dynamic of the group will vary depending on the nature of the participants.

Your goal as the Leader should be to foster understanding and familiarity with Scripture. For new believers or participants who are not comfortable with the Bible, your goal should be to help them get over that hurdle and begin to seek knowledge and understanding from His Word.

More mature participants will probably dig deeper to find personal meaning and understanding. They may particularly desire to discuss application questions and issues.

Prayer

Unless you have an outstanding person of prayer in your group, you as the leader should wrap up your discussion time with prayer that specifically reflects the discussion and the themes, purpose, and focus of the lesson.

Answers

Lesson 1 The Fundamentals of Obedience
Q1.
(a) Walk with Lord.
(b) By light of His Word.
(c) Do His good will.
Q2.
(a) He sheds glory on our way.
(b) He abides.
Q3.
(a) He can make things right – even with a smile.
(b) We should not doubt or fear if we abide in Him.
Q4.
(a) Give us favor.
(b) Give us joy.
Q5.
(a) Fellowship.
(b) Sit at His feet.
(c) Walk by His side.
Q6. Lay all on the altar.
Q7. Happy in Jesus.
Q8. n/a

Q9
John 14:15 If you love me, you will obey what I command.
John 14:23 Jesus replied, "If anyone loves me, he will obey my teaching . . ."
1 John 5:3 This is love for God: to obey his commands. . .
Q10.

Hebrews 5:8	Through suffering.
Philippians 2:8	Being humble.
John 15:10	Remaining in God's love.
Romans 1:5	Being faithful.
Ephesians 5:6	Fear of God's wrath.
John 14:15	Love for God.

Q11. n/a

Q12.
Proverbs 3:5-6
The basic foundational tenet: Do not rely on your own intelligence, but trust in the Lord. He will make it work!
Proverbs 28:9
It is considered an abomination to turn away from God's law. It is spiritually and morally an abomination to God.
Proverbs 19:20
We learn by accepting advice and instruction. Do not allow pride to cause you to ignore instruction that can make you wise.
Proverbs 1:7
Do not be foolish and ignore or reject wisdom that comes from instruction, particularly the "fear of the Lord" which is the foundation for gaining wisdom.
Proverbs 15:32
If you ignore instruction it is the equivalent of despising oneself. Rather listen to reproof in order to gain understanding.
Proverbs 10:8
Listen carefully to your teacher's instructions. Don't be babbling or whispering to others when you should be listening.
Proverbs 16:20
Trust in the Lord! Read, study, and examine God's word to gain understanding, wisdom, and blessing.
Proverbs 4:13
Instruction is very important. Ignore instruction and correction at your own risk.

Lesson 2 Is Obedience *REALLY* Required by God?
Q1.
No! Partial obedience is not acceptable to God. We are chosen for obedience.
Q2.
Yes! Peter is answering this question by indicating that we were chosen by God long ago and His Holy Spirit is sanctifying us in holiness and righteousness. Thus, "as a result" we are obedient. Paul confirms the intent for "the obedience of faith" for His sake to be demonstrated to all peoples (the nations).
Q3.
YES, obedience was a requirement from the beginning, and it was commanded for our own good!
Q4.
Jesus obeyed the Father and Jesus is to be our model.
Hebrews 5:8 *Although he was a son, he learned obedience through what he suffered.* ESV
Q5.
Our Parents:
Children are to obey parents!
Civil Authorities: Romans 13:1, 7
Citizens are to pay taxes and submit to authorities according to the established laws.

Church: Matthew 18:17

Followers are to obey church leaders.

Yes, obedience is expected with regard to normal activities and relationships. God never indicates that anything other than following His teaching is acceptable.

Q6.

It implies not only an emotional love but also a commitment of one's entire being to God's will and purposes. This type of love encompasses worship, reverence, and obedience to God. You can find this command originally in the Old Testament (Dt 6:5). It defines the most important responsibility of the disciple: love God completely.

Q7.

It requires empathy, compassion, and selflessness in our interactions with others, regardless of their background, beliefs, or circumstances. The commandment also appears in the Old Testament in Leviticus 19:18. The focus is on loving others selflessly.

Q8.

Unity! The Great Commandment emphasizes the importance of both love for God and love for others. It indicates that these two aspects of love and relationship are connected at the hip and form the foundation for having a right relationship with God.

Q9.

Obedience to this Commandment means we live our lives demonstrating love, kindness, and respect for both God and one another. It allows believers to make intelligent ethical decisions. God is worshipped and others are treated with dignity, goodness, and fairness, just like you would want to be treated.

Q10.

Practicing the requirements requires a transformation or circumcision of the heart. It challenges individuals to be humble by prioritizing love over selfish desires. And, in most people this will produce personal growth and spiritual maturity. But to be effective it must impact the core of one's being: the heart! "*Circumcision of the heart*" is a biblical metaphor that signifies a deep, inner transformation. Unlike physical circumcision, which is an external act, this refers to the spiritual process by which a person's heart is purified and made more receptive to God. This concept is mentioned in both the Old and New Testaments, such as Deuteronomy 10:16 and Romans 2:29, emphasizing the importance of inner spiritual change over mere external religious rituals.

Q11.

It should motivate believers to actively engage in acts of service, charity, and social justice. It compels disciples to work towards and for the well-being of others. Contrary to the prevailing secular opinion, self is not to be the primary focus of your life.

Q12.

Dt 6:4 and Lev 19:18 summarize God's commands on how to love God and one another. See Matthew 5:43-47 about loving your enemies and Mt 5:48 which ends the section saying to be perfect as the Father is perfect. This is consistent with the Law God gave Moses at Mt. Sinai and the messages and warning given by the Prophets.

Q13. Proverbs 3:6

Seeking God's will. Throughout the wisdom literature, there is an emphasis on seeking God's guidance in decision-making.

Proverbs 16:33 *The lot is cast into the lap, but its every decision is from the Lord.* ESV

Q14. Proverbs 12:22

Speak truthfully.

Proverbs frequently highlight the importance of honesty and integrity in interpersonal relationships.

Q15. Psalm 133:1

Unity and Fellowship

Finally, some Psalms emphasize the importance of unity and fellowship among believers. And, Psalm 55:13-14 describes the sweet fellowship among believers.

Q16. Ecclesiastes 5:18-20?

Be Content and Grateful

Ecclesiastes suggests that both contentment and gratitude are virtues.

DISCUSSION QUESTIONS

1. a. The Great Commandment – an absolute requirement.

b. The Great Commandment – an absolute requirement.

c. Required in order to have a right relationship with God.

d. Required in order to have a right relationship with God.

2. If "fearing God" is being in a right relationship, then obedience must automatically result.

3. Yes: One cannot be saved or have a right relationship with Jesus/God without strict adherence to what will gain those results.

No: Once saved, obedience is desired by God but not required to maintain salvation or His love.

Lesson 3 Obedience and Salvation

Q1

Obedience is absolutely necessary. But we are not told what the requirements are for life in these verses. Is the requirement faith, or is the requirement righteousness? Who is the audience in the above passages? Is the reference to Old or New Testament requirements? **LEADER:** You might ask your group, "Do you think there is enough information here to make a valid conclusion?"

Q2.

Philippians 2:14-15

Required: Do all things.

Result: Blameless and innocent child of God. . . light in the world.

Matthew 7:21-23

Required: Do the will of the Father.

Result: Enter the Kingdom.

Romans 2:13; Romans 6:16; Hebrews 5:9; Matthew 19:17

Required: Obedience.

Result: Justified; righteousness; eternal salvation; eternal life.

1 John 2:3-6

Required: Obedience (keep commandments); keep His word; walk as He walked.

Result: Know God (have a relationship); love of God perfected.

Mark 10:17-30

Exhortation: How difficult to enter the kingdom of God.

Required: Obey commandments.

Result: Eternal life.

Q3

Obedience appears to be a necessary requirement in every passage!

Q4

Ephesians 2:8-9

Salvation is a gift from God received through faith in Jesus Christ. It is not earned by our works, but rather given by God's grace.

Luke 14:25-33

Salvation is free, but it also requires a commitment to follow Christ wholeheartedly. That means a relationship with family is secondary to Christ (thus the word "hate") and all things should be considered (count the cost) because Jesus becomes the number 1 commitment.

Acts 2:38

Acknowledging our sinfulness and turning away (repentance) from it is necessary for salvation.

Romans 10:9-10

We must confess that Jesus is Lord and believe in our hearts (inner being) that God raised Him from the dead.

Mark 16:16

Baptism is an important, but not necessary, part of salvation. It symbolizes our identification with Christ's death, burial, and resurrection. Based on other Scriptures baptism is an act of love and obedience, after being saved, not a requirement for salvation.

1 John 2:3-6

A new life in Christ calls for obedience to God's commands. As followers of Jesus, we strive to live according to His teachings. It would be very difficult to believe a person was saved who ignores or rejects the teachings of Christ.

Q5.

John 3:16; Romans 10:9; Titus 3:5

Salvation is a gift of God's grace, freely offered to all who believe in Jesus Christ as Lord and Savior (John 3:16, Romans 10:9). It is not earned or merited by human works or obedience to the law (Titus 3:5).

Q6.

James 2:17

While obedience is not the basis for salvation, it is often presented as evidence of genuine faith and a relationship with God. Jesus teaches that those who love Him will obey His commands (John 14:15), and James writes that faith without works is dead (James 2:17). Genuine faith produces a transformed life characterized by obedience to God's will and commands.

Q7.

Matthew 24:13 and **Hebrews 10:36**

The New Testament encourages believers to persevere in faith and obedience, enduring in their commitment to Christ to the end. Salvation is a lifelong journey of faithfulness and obedience to God.

Q8.

1 John 1:9

The New Testament teaches that believers who have sinned can experience restoration and renewal through confession and repentance. If we confess our sins, God is faithful to cleanse us from those sins (even all unrighteousness). Praise God!

Q9.

John 10:27-29

Jesus says His sheep hear His voice and will follow Him; He gives them eternal life; and they will <u>never</u> perish. No one can snatch them out of His hand. This would seem to indicate that even serious problems will ultimately be overcome.

Romans 8:38-39

Paul asserts that nothing can separate believers from the love of God in Christ Jesus. This includes a long list of things. It certainly appears that Paul is making the point that nothing of any kind can separate a believer from Christ.

CONSEQUENCES

Separation For Not Knowing God

2 Thessalonians 1:9 *T*

Here those who are unbelievers and do not accept the gospel will suffer the punishment of eternal destruction, away from the presence of the Lord and from the glory of His might.

Consequences of Sin

Romans 6:23

The New Testament affirms that the wages of sin is death. Persistent rejection to God's requirements for salvation leads to spiritual death and separation from Him, as well as negative consequences in this life, such as broken relationships, guilt, and spiritual emptiness.

Judgment and Wrath For Hardened Hearts

Romans 2:5

The New Testament warns of the coming judgment and wrath of God upon those who persist in disobedience and <u>unbelief</u>.

Eternal Punishment For Lack of Compassion

Matthew 25:46

The New Testament teaches that those who reject the gospel of Jesus and persist in unbelief will face eternal punishment and condemnation.

All Will be Judged

2 Corinthians 5:10

The New Testament emphasizes that <u>all</u> people will give an account to God for their actions and choices. We must all appear before the judgment seat of Christ: the unbeliever for the sin of unbelief and the believer for his works, both good and bad. Note, that the judgment on the believer is not a salvation judgment.

Exclusion From the Kingdom For the Unrighteous

1 Corinthians 6:9-10

Here Paul warns that the unrighteous will not inherit the kingdom of God and lists various sinful behaviors as reasons for exclusion. We must attain righteousness to be present with God and the only righteousness available to the sinner is Jesus.

Lesson 4 Punishment For Disobedience

Q1.

2 Thessalonians 1:8

God will punish us for both not knowing Him and knowing but not being obedient to the gospel.

Ephesians 5:6

God's wrath is meted out to the disobedient, even to those that have been deceived by others.

1 Peter 4:17

Judgment is not just for unbelievers and Peter says here it should <u>start</u> with the family of God. Such punishment should be a sign to unbelievers that their punishment will be worse.

2 Corinthians 10:5-6

Nothing is more important or more powerful than the Word of God and the gospel. All things are subject to the rule of Christ. Disobedience will be punished.

Q2.

Hebrews 12:5-11

This passage indicates that God disciplines those He loves, just as a good father disciplines his children. The discipline of God is intended for the good of believers, to produce holiness and righteousness in their lives. It may involve correction, rebuke, or hardship designed to turn believers away from their disobedience. Notice verse 11 refers to be "trained" by discipline.

1 Corinthians 3:12-15

While believers are saved by grace they may suffer loss of rewards for disobedience or unfaithfulness. This is an example of a judgment on believers' works, with some works being burned up as worthless, resulting in loss of reward. It does <u>not</u> impact salvation.

1 Corinthians 11:29-30

Disobedience to God's commands can lead to harsh consequences in this life, such as suffering, illness, or the loss of blessings. Some believers in the Corinthian church had become weak and sick, and some had even died, because of their unworthy participation in the Lord's Supper.

Galatians 6:1

Paul instructs believers to restore those who are involved in sin with a spirit of gentleness, seeking to bring them back into the Christian community with other believers.

Matthew 18:15-17

In cases of persistent or unrepentant sin, the New Testament provides for the discipline of believers, including exclusion from fellowship in the church. Here Jesus describes a process for dealing with sin within the church, resulting in the removal of the unrepentant individual from the church.

Q3.

Continuing Sin: Romans 6:1-2

This passage emphasizes that those believers, set free from the power of sin by Christ's death and resurrection, are called to live lives characterized by obedience to God rather than continuing in a pattern of sin. To suggest that believers can sin without worrying about retribution or punishment is nonsense, just like suggesting if we sin then God can display His grace.

Sins of the Flesh: Galatians 5:19-21

In this passage, Paul contrasts the works of the flesh, which include acts of disobedience and sinful behavior, with the fruit of the Spirit. He warns that those who persist in practicing such things will not inherit the kingdom of God. Believers must turn away (repent) of these types of activities.

Sexual Immorality and Idolatry: Ephesians 5:5-6 and Colossians 3:5-6

Paul cautions the Ephesian believers against participating in immoral practices and idolatry, stating that those who do so will experience the wrath of God and not inherit the kingdom of Christ and God. Paul exhorts the Colossian believers to put to death sinful practices, including disobedience, because such behavior incurs God's wrath.

Intentional Sin: Hebrews 10:26-31 and James 4:17

The author in Hebrews issues a stern warning against willful sinning and disobedience, emphasizing that those who persist in such behavior are in danger of facing the severe judgment from God. James also emphasizes the importance of obedience to God's commands and underscores the responsibility believers have to act in accordance with God's will and instructions.

Backsliding: 2 Peter 2:20-22

Peter warns about the danger of returning to a life of sin and disobedience after experiencing and knowing the knowledge of the truth. He describes the dire consequences of such behavior, comparing it to a dog returning to its vomit or a washed pig returning to wallow in the mud. The inference here is that sin has a strong and almost unbreakable grasp on our lives.

MORE SERIOUS WARNINGS

I Never Knew You: Matthew 7:21-23

Jesus warns about the danger of professing faith but not living in obedience to God's will. The statement that Jesus never knew the individual speaks strongly to the requirement of a relationship. Just performing great works will not cut it. He states clearly that not everyone who calls Him "Lord" will enter the kingdom of heaven, but only those who do the will of His Father in heaven. God's desire is for our faith and a relationship.

Rejection of the Faith: 1 Timothy 4:1-2

Paul warns Timothy about the dangers of false teachings that lead people away from the truth. He cautions that some will leave the faith and follow deceiving spirits and even the teachings of demons. Such activities lead to disobedience and departure from God's truth and increase the ease to reject the faith, reject Jesus, and fall into apostasy.

Idolatry: 1 Corinthians 10:7-12

Paul reminds the Corinthian believers of the Israelites' example in the wilderness, warning them not to follow in their disobedient footsteps. He emphasizes that these things were written as warnings for believers, urging them to heed the lessons and avoid falling into disobedience and idolatry. Things that become more important than God become idols.

Obedience is the Proof: 1 John 2:3-6

John emphasizes the connection between obedience to God's commands and a genuine relationship with Him. He states that those who claim to know God but do not obey His commands are liars, but those who obey God's word demonstrate their love for Him and live in union with Him.

CONCLUSION

LEADER: You may ask your group if there are any warnings about sin that they want to talk about that were not covered in this lesson. For example:

Even what he has will be taken from him.	Mk 4:25
Go sell everything you have.	Mk 10:21-22
There will be tribulation for every soul that does evil.	Ro 2:8-9
If your right hand causes you to sin, cut it off.	Mt 5:30
I am about to spit you out of my mouth.	Rev 3:16

Lesson 5 The Need for Christ

Q1.

1 John 5:3

His commands or requirements are not burdensome. They are not hard, oppressive, or severe.

John 15:10

Obedience is a necessary requirement to be in a love relationship with Christ.

Galatians 2:16-21

Obedience is not a requirement for salvation. It occurs because a disciple is grateful for God's grace and wants to show God's love to others.

Q2.

Romans 3:23

Sin: Romans 3:23 teaches that all have sinned and fall short of the glory of God. Sin separates humanity from God, resulting in spiritual death and condemnation (see Romans 6:23).

Ephesians 2:8-9

FAITH (not works): We do not have the ability to save ourselves. Despite our best efforts to obey God's commands, we are unable to save ourselves or earn salvation through perfection. Our sinful nature prevents us from fully obeying God's law and living up to His standards of righteousness.

GRACE: Salvation is not earned through obedience to the law but is received as a gift of God's grace through faith in Christ. His obedience and sacrifice provide the basis for our salvation, and we are justified by faith in Him apart from works of the law (Romans 3:28).

Matthew 5:17

The Law: Jesus came to fulfill the righteous requirements of God's law on behalf of humanity. He lived a perfect, sinless life, fulfilling the law's demands and offering Himself as the perfect sacrifice for man's sin (Hebrews 9:14). Jesus demonstrated His ability to live according to the Law, while all of Israel's attempts failed.

1 Peter 2:24

Atonement: Through His death on the cross, Jesus atoned for the sins of humanity, paying the penalty for our rebellion, thus being the means of reconciling us to God (Romans 5:8). His sacrifice satisfied the justice of God and made forgiveness and salvation available to all who believe in Him.

Galatians 5:22-23

Fruit: Through faith in Jesus Christ, believers receive the indwelling presence of the Holy Spirit, who empowers us to live obedient lives and conform to the image of Christ (Galatians 5:16). The Spirit produces fruit in the lives of true believers.

Q3.

Ephesians 1:13-14

Indwelling Presence: The Holy Spirit dwells believers as the seal and guarantee of their salvation. The Spirit's presence enables believers to abide with God, receive His guidance, and experience His empowering presence, resulting in obedience.

John 16:13

Guidance: The Holy Spirit guides believers into all truth, helping them understand and apply God's Word to their lives.

John 16:8

Conviction of Sin: The Holy Spirit convicts believers of sin, righteousness, and judgment. By revealing the truth of God's standards and convicting hearts of disobedience, the Spirit moves believers to repentance and obedience.

Titus 3:5

Romans 12:2

Regeneration and Renewal: The Holy Spirit regenerates believers, transforming their hearts and minds to conform to the likeness of Christ. Through this process of sanctification, the Holy Spirit gradually empowers believers to live in obedience to God's commands.

1 Corinthians 2:12-13

Revelation: The Holy Spirit illuminates the Scriptures, helping followers understand and apply God's Word. By providing spiritual insight and wisdom, the Spirit directs believers in the path of righteousness.

Acts 1:8

Empowerment: The Holy Spirit empowers believers for effective service and ministry. Through our spiritual gifts and the fruit of the Spirit, believers are equipped to fulfill their God-given purposes and bear witness to Christ in the world.

Romans 8:26-27

Intercession: The Holy Spirit intercedes for believers in their weakness, helping them with their prayers and interceding for them according to God's will. The Spirit strengthens believers in times of temptation and trial, enabling them to persevere in obedience.

Lesson 6 The Fear Of The Lord

Q1.

Matthew 5:20

Jesus teaches that true discipleship involves a righteousness that exceeds mere outward adherence to religious laws. It involves a righteousness of the heart that is rooted in love for God and others.

Romans 6:13

Paul exhorts believers to live in righteousness by offering themselves fully to God, allowing Him to transform their lives and actions.

Ephesians 4:24

Believers are called to put on a new self, which is characterized by "true righteousness and holiness." This involves living in accordance with God's standards rather than conforming to the patterns of the world.

Q2.

Deuteronomy 6:2

Keeping God decrees and commands allows for the fear of the Lord to develop, particularly in children who must be taught about their faith.

Deuteronomy 10:12-13

Note that in the "list" of five requirements that obedience occurs twice: (1) walk in his ways, and (2) observe the Lord's commands and decrees. Obviously obedience is important to God.

Psalms 128:1

In Ps 128 the implication is that you are blessed and that the definition of fearing is walking in his ways.

Psalms 111:10

Ps 111 associates obedience with having good understanding.

Psalms 103:17-18

Those who keep God's covenant (obey) have the love of God with them, and that is even extended to the children of those who obey.

DISCUSSION QUESTIONS

1. The phrase "the whole duty of man" reflects back on the meaning and purpose of life. By stating that the "whole duty of man" is to fear God and keep His commandments, Solomon emphasized the ultimate purpose and responsibility of humanity. It suggests that true fulfillment and meaning in life are found in aligning oneself with God's purposes and living in accordance with His will. This perspective counters the fleeting pursuits of pleasure, wealth, and wisdom that Solomon explored throughout the book of Ecclesiastes, ultimately pointing to a life centered on God as the source of true fulfillment and significance.

2. Fear of God provides the foundational motivation for obedience, while keeping His commandments represents the practical outworking of that reverence in daily life. Together, they form the basis for a life of meaningful devotion to God and faithful adherence to His will.

3. *Who will be judged?* <All>

Ro 14:12 *So then, <u>each of us</u> will give an account of himself to God.* NIV

2 Cor 5:10 *For we must <u>all appear</u> before the judgment seat of Christ, that each one may receive what is due him for the things done while in the body, whether good or bad.* NIV

Who is the judge? <Jesus>

Jn 5:22 . . . *the Father judges no one, but has entrusted all judgment to the Son*

What is judged? <Believers works>

1 Cor 3:11-15 *For no one can lay any foundation other than the one already laid, which is Jesus Christ. If any man builds on this foundation using gold, silver, costly stones, wood, hay or straw, his work will be shown for what it is. . . It will be revealed with fire, and the fire will test the quality of each man's work. If what he has built survives, he will receive his reward. If it is burned up, he will suffer loss; he himself will be saved, but only as one escaping through the flames. [Note: Salvation is not in question here.]*

Lesson 7 Benefits of Obedience

Q1.

Romans 1:5

Hebrews 5:9

I am saved by the obedience of faith (1:5) and I must obey Him (5:9).

Q2.

John 14:15, 21, 23

2 John 6

We have a <u>love</u> relationship with Christ if we live according to his commands. Love produces obedience. It does not say that obedience produces love. This concept is very important for followers to understand.

Q3.
John 13:34
We are to <u>love</u> one another. A new command is to love <u>just as Jesus loves us.</u>
Q4.
1 John 2:3-4, 6
I am to <u>know</u> Jesus.
LEADER: You might ask the leading question: "Why is 'knowing' Jesus important? What passages(s) could you identify where not knowing Jesus or Jesus not knowing you is important?" See Mt 7:21-23; Lk 13:25-27; Mt 25:11-12. These passages highlight the sobering reality that merely professing to know Jesus is not enough. True discipleship involves knowing Him intimately and living in obedience to His teachings. A relationship exists.
Q5.
John 8:31
1 John 1:4-6
I have a right relationship with Him and that includes:
Jn 8:31: Living under the instruction of God's Word.
1 Jn 1: Be open to the truth and the light because God/Jesus is Light.
We cannot claim a real relationship or to be a disciple and live in disobedience (darkness).
Q6.
John 15:10
1 John 3:24
I abide (remain) in Him.
LEADER: You might ask the group, "What does it mean to abide or remain?" In John 15:10, Jesus says, *"If you keep my commands, you will abide in my love, just as I have kept my Father's commands and abide in his love"* (NIV). The term "abide" in this context carries important significance. To abide in Jesus is to live in close relationship with Him, to be obedient to His commands, and to experience the fullness of His love and presence in our lives. It's a dynamic, ongoing process of growing deeper in our relationship with Him and allowing His life to flow through us.
Q7.
John 15:14
I am a friend of Jesus (God) if I am obedient. **LEADER:** You might ask your group if they can identify any specific people in the Bible who were identified as friends of God.
Two men were called friends of God: Abraham and Moses. In addition both David and Enoch had very close relationships with God, but were not directly referred to as friends.
Several individuals are noted for having "walked" with God, signifying their close relationship and intimate fellowship with Him: Enoch (Gen 5:24), Noah (Gen 6:9), Abraham (Gen 24:40), and Isaac (Gen 48:15). These individuals are esteemed in Scripture for their devotion, faithfulness, and intimate communion with God.
Q8.
1 John 3:22-23
3:22 We receive answers to prayer – even anything we want!
3:23 <u>But</u> we must believe in Jesus and love one another.

Q9.

Luke 11:28

I am blessed. **LEADER:** You might ask your group, "What kind of blessings might be in view here?" One obvious result is that God is actively working in our lives.

Q10.

2 Thessalonians 1:8

Ephesians 5:6

I will escape or avoid punishment [flaming fire (hell); God's wrath]

Q11.

Deuteronomy 28:1-10

Obedience to God's commands in the OT resulted in divine blessings, including protection, and provision. Here God promises blessing after blessing to the Israelites if they obey His commands. **LEADER:** It might be interesting to have your group identify the similar or corresponding blessings that might be received today for obedience.

Genesis 39:2-6

Obedience to God's commands can lead to favor with God and with others. Joseph found favor with Potiphar, his Egyptian master, because of his obedience and integrity. Similarly, throughout the Old Testament, individuals who obeyed God's commands often found favor with God and with those around them.

Psalms 119:165

Obedience to God's commands can lead to great peace in personal and community life.

Psalm 91:9-12

Obedience to God's commands can produce protection from harm and enemies. The psalmist declares that those who make the Lord their refuge and dwell in His shelter will be protected from danger and harm. That is a common theme in the Old Testament.

Joshua 21:45

Obedience to God's commands can lead to the fulfillment of His promises. When the Israelites obeyed God's commands and followed His guidance, they experienced the fulfillment of God's promises, including the inheritance of the Promised Land.

Daniel 12:2-3

Obedience to God's commands is associated with blessings and rewards that extend beyond this life. Here Daniel speaks of the resurrection of the dead and the reward for those who are wise and lead others to righteousness. Obedience to God's commands is seen as leading to spiritual rewards and blessings in the life to come.

Q12.

John 14:23

Obedience to God's commands deepens the believer's relationship with Him. Jesus says that obedience will lead to intimacy with God the Father, as believers experience His presence and fellowship in their lives.

2 Peter 1:5-8

Obedience to God's commands leads to spiritual growth and maturity. Here believers are encouraged to add certain qualities to their faith. Obedience will produce spiritual fruit in the believer's life.

John 8:31-32
Obedience brings freedom from the power of sin and breaks the bondage of sin which enables believers to live in freedom and righteousness.

John 15:10-11
Obedience to God's commands brings fulfillment to the believer's life and leads to a deep sense of joy that comes from abiding in His love.

1 John 3:22
Obedience enhances the believer's prayer life and aligns the believer's desires with God's will, making prayers more effective and in accordance with His purposes.

Philippians 2:2-4
Obedience fosters harmony among believers. Here Paul urges believers to be like-minded. Obedience to the command to love one another and to serve one another promotes unity within the body of Christ.

Matthew 19:29
Obedience to God's commands results in eternal rewards and inheritance in the kingdom of God. Obedience, even in the midst of sacrifice or persecution, leads to blessings and rewards in the life to come.

Lesson 8 Standing Firm
Q1. (1) Earthly activities and values that were previously mentioned; (2) temporal things rather than the future; (3) worldly accomplishments versus being right with God, (4) having goals or purposes based on the values of the world.

Q2. – Q7. n/a

Q8.

John 8:31 – Jesus is emphasizing that disciples will follow His teaching. Obedience is expected. This is not an issue of salvation.

Luke 21:19 – Again verse is emphasizing the importance of standing firm. The implication is that we may not gain life if we do not stand firm.

1 Corinthians 15:2 – This verse may confirm the concept that failure to stand firm can make our faith in vain, but it can also relate to those who are not true believers.

Lesson 9 Examples of Biblical Obedience
Q1. .Both, they really can't be separated. God was testing Abraham's obedience which would reflect the degree or nature of his commitment to the "fear of the Lord."

Q2. Total commitment to their God. Truly knowing God.

Q3.

Acts 14:5-7, 19-20 (Lystra and Derbe): While preaching in Lystra, Paul and Barnabas faced opposition from unbelieving Jews, who stoned Paul and left him for dead. However, he miraculously survived.

Acts 16:19-40 (Philippi): In Philippi, Paul and Silas were arrested after casting out a spirit of divination from a slave girl. They were severely beaten and thrown into prison. Despite their imprisonment, they praised God, and miraculously, an earthquake shook the prison doors open. When the jailer discovered that the prisoners had not escaped, he asked Paul and Silas what he must do to be saved. Paul and Silas then shared the Gospel with him and his household, leading to their conversion.

Acts 21:27-36 (Jerusalem): In Jerusalem, Paul faced opposition from the Jews who accused him of defiling the temple by bringing Gentiles into it. A riot ensued, and Paul was seized by the crowd and dragged out of the temple. The Roman commander intervened and arrested Paul to prevent him from being killed by the mob.

Acts 9:23-25 (Damascus): After his conversion, Paul (then known as Saul) began preaching boldly in Damascus about Jesus being the Son of God. However, his preaching angered the Jews, who plotted to kill him. The plot became so serious that the disciples had to lower Paul in a basket through an opening in the city wall to help him escape. This escape demonstrated Paul's obedience to the Holy Spirit in continuing his mission despite the danger and his willingness to take unconventional measures to ensure his safety.

Q4. Job was not patient! In fact he lost his patience. But he did not give up, meaning he persevered.

Q5. and **Q6** n/a

(1) Holman (HSCB) study note says "turning over to Satan" was a common way of saying excommunication. (2) He was not going to do anything that would prevent Satan from selling him lies. (3) It's a reference to church discipline in that Paul had done all he could – Hymenaeus was now on his own. (4) If one is "out of the church" then it is far easier for Satan to get a foothold in your life. (5) NOTE: 1 Cor 5:5 *you are to deliver this man to Satan for the destruction of the flesh, so that his spirit may be saved in the day of the Lord.* ESV

Q7. He had (1) deviated from the truth; (2) some kind of error in his thinking . . . it often starts with little steps, until you find yourself a long ways away! (3) The issue may have been His thinking about the resurrection which would have been a very serious issue for Paul; (4) maybe he intended to imply he was not looking to reject the truth, but just not paying attention and wandered away.

DISCUSSION QUESTIONS

1. Ways include: (1) taking a stand for righteousness; (2) doing what is right regardless of consequences; (3) standing firm in both word and deed; or (4) calling out a friend who has wandered from the faith.

2. Unwavering; not stop to consider disobedience; intentionality; strong spiritual character.

3. n/a

4. Follow the advice given in Joshua 1:6-7: "Be strong and very courageous . . . " This advice is repeated in Dt 316-7, 23; Joshua 10:25; 1 Sam 4:9; 2 Sam 2:7; 1 Chron 22:13, 28:20; Ps 27:14, 31:24; Isa 35:4; Haggai 2:4; 1 Cor 16:13; Eph 6:10. The frequency of this advice should be instructive.

5. If we are strong/courageous, God is faithful and will supply are every need.

6. In almost all of the examples the impact went far beyond just the primary person involved.

7. We may never understand the influence or ultimate impact of our obedience in this lifetime.

Lesson 10 – Summary n/a

Free PDF
MAKE WISE DECISIONS

[Get the ebook version for 99 cents]

Consequences Shape Lives.

This book discusses the nature of decisions and explores eight essential questions to make better decisions.

You are a few decisions away from transforming your life. You can make better decisions! This resource has sections on what makes a poor decision, questions to ask yourself, traps to avoid, short and sweet decisions, the wise decision framework, and twenty ways to be wise. It also has a handy decision-making checklist. (12 pages)

Free PDF: https://getwisdompublishing.com/resource-registration/

Kindle ebook for 99 cents: https://www.amazon.com/dp/B0FG8NC53J

Ebook

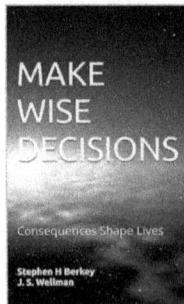

MAKE WISE DECISIONS

Consequences Shape Lives

Stephen H Berkey
J. S. Wellman

Free PDF

Ten Steps to Wise Choices

Timeless Wisdom. Practical Tools. Lasting Impact.

Free PDF
Life Improvement Principles

[Get the ebook version for 99 cents]

You can live your best life!

Welcome to a journey of discovery! In case you have forgotten, your actions have consequences. Unlock your potential! This book (60+ pages) provides the overview of all our strategies and wisdom principles to live your best life. You *can* transform your life! Get your wisdom-based roadmap to a better life and unlock all the possibilities for growth and success.

Free PDF: https://getwisdompublishing.com/resource-registration/

Kindle ebook for 99 cents:
https://www.amazon.com/dp/B0FG883KZM

Ebook

Life Improvement Principles

You can live your best life!

Stephen H Berkey
J. S. Wellman

Free PDF

Make it your life goal to be the best you can be!

Discover Wisdom and live the life you deserve.

Walk in all the ways the Lord has commanded!

What Next?

Continue Your Journey

Continue Study in the *Jesus Follower* Series
The Jesus Follower Bible Study Series
https://www.amazon.com/dp/B0DHP39P5J

Be Challenged by the *OBSCURE* Series
The *OBSCURE* Bible Study Series
https://www.amazon.com/dp/B08T7TL1B1

Tackle Wisdom-Driven Life Change
Apply Biblical Wisdom to Live Your Best Life!
"Effective Life Change"
https://www.amazon.com/dp/1952359732

Know What You Should Pray
Personal Daily Prayer Guide
https://www.amazon.com/What-Should-Pray-Personal-Journal/dp/1952359260/

Decide to be the Very Best You Can Be
The Life Planning Series
https://www.amazon.com/dp/B09TH9SYC4

You Can Help:

SOCIAL MEDIA: Mention The Jesus Follower Bible Study Series on your social platforms. Include the hashtag #jesusbiblestudy so we are aware of your post.

FRIENDS: Recommend this series to your family, friends, small group, Sunday School class leaders, or your church.

REVIEW: Please give us your honest review at
https://www.amazon.com/dp/1952359643

Walk in all the ways the Lord has commanded!

The OBSCURE Bible Study Series
Continue your journey through the hidden wisdom of Scripture with the OBSCURE Series.

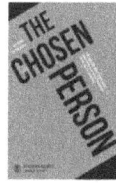

Blasphemy, Grace, Quarrels & Reconciliation: The lives of first-century disciples.
This book presents Joseph of Arimathea, Joanna, Ananias, Hymenaeus, and Cornelius (a centurion). It illustrates the nature and challenges of life as a first-century disciple.

The Beginning and the End: From creation to eternity.
This book has four lessons from Genesis and four from Revelation covering creation, rebellion, grace, worship, and eternity. God is leading us to worship in the Throne Room.

God at the Center: He is sovereign and I am not.
This book examines the virgin birth, worship, prayer, the sovereignty of God, compromise, and trust. God is at the center of all these stories. He is at the center of our lives.

Women of Courage: God did some serious business with these women.
This book examines the lives of Jael, Rizpah, the woman of Tekoa, Tabitha, Shiphrah, and Lydia. These women exhibit great courage and faithfulness. God used them in amazing ways.

The Beginning of Wisdom: Your personal character counts.
In this book we find courage, loyalty, thankfulness, love, forgiveness, and humility. Personal character counts. Decisions have consequences. Wisdom will help us stand firm in our faith.

Miracles & Rebellion: The good, the bad, and the indifferent.
God hates sin and loves to heal the faithful. The rebellion of Korah, Haman, and Alexander compare to the healing stories of Aeneas, a slave girl, and the crippled man at Lystra.

The Chosen People: There is a remnant.
This book concentrates mostly on Israel in the Old Testament, but also covers some interesting subjects as Lucifer, Michael the archangel, and Job's wife.

The Chosen Person: Keep your eyes on Jesus.
The focus is on Jesus and the superiority of Christ. We investigate Melchizedek, the disciples on the road to Emmaus, Nicodemus, and the criminal on the cross.

WEBSITE: http://getwisdompublishing.com/products/
AMAZON: www.amazon.com/author/stephenhberkey

Life Planning Series

Read these books if you want to live a better life.
The primary audience for this series is the secular self-help market,
but the concepts are Christian based.

CHOOSE FAITH	**For the spiritual seeker and those with spiritual questions.** *Your Spiritual Guidebook For Questions About Religion, God, Heaven, Truth, Evil, and the Afterlife.* **https://www.amazon.com/dp/1952359473**
CHOOSE CORE VALUES	**Core values will drive your life.** **https://www.amazon.com/dp/195235949X**

Other Titles in the Life Planning Series
CHOOSE Integrity
CHOOSE Friends Wisely
CHOOSE The Right Words
CHOOSE Good Work Habits
CHOOSE Financial Responsibility
CHOOSE A Positive Self-Image
CHOOSE Leadership
CHOOSE Love and Family
LIFE PLANNING HANDBOOK A Life Plan Is The Key To Personal Growth https://www.amazon.com/gp/product/1952359325

Go to:

https://www.amazon.com/dp/B09TH9SYC4

to get your copy.

Personal Daily Prayer Guide
Prayer Resource and Journal

This is a great resource to kick-start your prayer life!

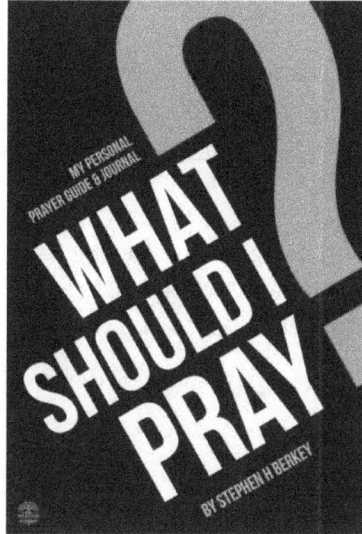

Know what to pray.
Pray based on Bible verses.
Strengthen your prayer life.
Access reference resources.
Pray with eternal implications.
Write your own prayers if desired.
Organize and focus your prayer time.
Learn what the Bible says about prayer.
Find encouragement and advice on how to pray.
Reduce frustration and distraction in your prayer time.

Get your copy today!

https://www.amazon.com/What-Should-Pray-Personal-Journal/dp/1952359260/

Acknowledgments

My wife has patiently persevered while I indulged my interest in writing. Thank you for all your help and assistance.

Our older daughter has been an invaluable resource. She has also graciously produced our website at www.getwisdompublishing.com

Our middle daughter designed the covers for most of my books, but I gave her a vacation on this Series. We are very grateful for her help, talent and creativity.

Notes

1 OBEDIENCE: from The New Unger's Bible Dictionary.

2 OBEDIENCE: from Nelson's Illustrated Bible Dictionary.

3 OBEDIENCE: from International Standard Bible Encyclopedia.

About the Author

Steve attended church as a child and accepted Christ when he was 10 years old. But his walk with Jesus left a lot to be desired for the next 44 years. In 1994 he "wrestled" with God for some period of months and in September of that year totally surrendered his life to Jesus.

In 1996 he was so driven to study God's Word that he attended the Indianapolis campus of Trinity Evangelical Divinity School (Chicago) to earn a Certificate of Biblical Studies. His hunger for God's Word led him to lead and write all his own Bible studies for his small group. He has been a Bible study leader for the past 25 years.

After 25 years as an actuary, and 20 years as an entrepreneur, he began his third career as an author in 2020, when he published The OBSCURE Bible Study Series. The Jesus Follower Bible Study Series was completed in early 2025. He is a member of The Church at Station Hill in Spring Hill, TN, a regional campus of Brentwood Baptist (Brentwood TN).

"Get Wisdom Publishing is dedicated to being the trusted source of wisdom-driven books that inspire growth, guide decisions, and empower readers to live with purpose and fulfillment."

Contact Us

Website: www.getwisdompublishing.com

Email: info@getwisdompublishing.com

Facebook: Get Wisdom Publishing

Author's Page:
www.amazon.com/author/stephenhberkey

Amazon's Jesus Follower Bible Study Series page:
https://www.amazon.com/dp/B0DHP39P5J

"Go beyond devotionals.
Experience biblical wisdom in action!"

GET**WISDOM**
PUBLISHING

www.ingramcontent.com/pod-product-compliance
Lightning Source LLC
Chambersburg PA
CBHW060320050426
42449CB00011B/2578